HAND BOOK FOR SPIRITUAL SURVIVAL

HAND BOOK FOR SPIRITUAL SURVIVAL

Peter E. Gillquist
author of LOVE IS NOW

ZONDERVAN
PUBLISHING HOUSE

OF THE ZONDERVAN CORPORATION | GRAND RAPIDS, MICHIGAN 49506

HANDBOOK FOR SPIRITUAL SURVIVAL
Formerly published as: *Farewell to the Fake I.D.*

© 1971 by Zondervan Publishing House
Grand Rapids, Michigan

Library of Congress Catalog Card Number 72-168649

First printing of Zondervan
   Books edition   January 1973
Second printing September 1973

Unless otherwise indicated, Scripture quotations are from the *Modern Language Bible — The New Berkeley Version in Modern English,* copyright © 1945, 1959, 1969, used by permission of Zondervan Publishing House, Grand Rapids, Michigan.

Printed in the United States of America

To all who dwell
in the City of good abode.

CONTENTS

Prologue

Writing a book is a unique experience.

You write because there are so many things you really want to say. There are things that have come through your experience (in my case, my experience with Jesus Christ) that you just want to expose. There is a story to tell that you genuinely feel will help those who read, even though you know what you say is incomplete, and that God has *yet to show* you many things.

But there is another side of it,

In many ways, this book has been difficult to write. The reader will catch this far fewer times than I because I have lived it. There are some things I have felt compelled to say that are a put-down to a segment of what is happening today under the assumed signature of God. I have said these things because I have a staunch awareness that they need to be said.

There are things I say which might deface me. They are strong; and to one not closely associated with the current **realm of spiritual warfare, they will make little impact. How-**

ever, I have chosen to write of strong truths which reflect my present involvement, rather than to dilute them and give false security to the masses whom the world calls "religious." You risk misunderstandings when you let loose with what you really believe because it may not be acceptable—even to your brethren who may not understand the context out of which you speak.

In some instances, I have dealt more heavily with *issues* than I usually do. However, these are matters related strongly to our times; thus, I stand in peace with what I have said.

I feel at ease in submitting this manuscript for publication. It reveals, as clearly as I am able to state, the workings of the Lord within me. I am eager to learn if others will identify with the portions of His Word which He has so deliberately exposed to me.

Regarding acknowledgments, I wish to mention several who have helped most graciously in moving the book through its early stages. Miss Susan Crawford, our alumni editor at Memphis State University, got me off the starting blocks by reading the initial manuscript and motioning me on, and Gordon Walker and Ray and Eunice Nethery were of tremendous help in editing. Mrs. John Dold of Wilmette, Illinois, typed the final draft under the pressure of the publisher's deadline.

Between then and now, my partner in oneness, Marilyn, and two others, Dr. Herbert Lee Williams, chairman of the journalism department at Memphis State University, and E. Fred Alexander, a comrade in the field of development and a devoted student of the Word of God, gave most helpful suggestions on the final proofs.

Try these truths on in your own spirit. See if they witness to something that God is doing in you. He has created a rumble in me and I had to let it flow.

Sometimes You Have to Rap

There is a fruitlessness that happens on earth.
— King Solomon

1

Sometimes You Have to Rap

The termination of World War II (as I recall experiencing it from the vantage point of a seven-year-old) brought *so* many changes.

Bubble gum was back. Whereas before the corner druggist would limit us to two pieces, now we could buy all we wanted.

Car tires got better, too. I can still remember the men talking at family dinners on Sunday afternoons about how great it was to be able to replace their synthetic rubber tires with real ones.

And comic books returned. Captain Marvel, Plastic Man and Wonder Woman seemed to be back in business to stay.

There was a section in some of the comic books which I always read. It usually appeared on either the inside or the outside of the back cover.

It was the Charles Atlas ad, and the ads were all the same. The headline would read: "Are You Tired of Being a Six-Foot,

Ninety-Pound Weakling?" Then eight or nine successive frames would show the travails of a man who was tall and skinny. If you are old enough, you can probably still picture the sequence. In the first frame, our man and his girl are sunbathing on the beach. Then a huge, well-developed bully comes by, kicks sand in the face of the lesser man, and ends up with the chick. I still laugh to myself as I think of the next picture where our skinny friend kicks over a chair in his dingy bachelor bedroom and admits out loud, "I'm tired of being a six-foot, ninety-pound weakling!" He sends in the Charles Atlas coupon and goes to work on the dynamic tension program for physical build-up.

Six weeks later, we are back on the beach. Our frail friend has now become a human specimen who would rival the monster man of the Green Bay Packers. The bully appears again to check out the girl, but after receiving a sharp right to his jaw, he makes a strategic withdrawal into the crowd on the beach to avoid further trouble.

I read through that ad so often, I knew it by heart. *But I still kept on reading it.* It wasn't just the physical thing of being muscle-bound that attracted me (though I must admit that I sent for the booklet!); it was the idea of being able to handle the circumstances surrounding me. And as I worked up the courage to admit to my friends that I read the ad, I discovered that virtually all of them read it too.

There is something about being a winner, an overcomer, that really attracts people. No one likes to get whipped. And though I did not realize it at the time, there was something within me — even at the age of seven or eight — that wanted to excell.

I shall never forget the exhilaration of an early spring afternoon in my junior year of high school. The year before I had been bedridden by a serious illness which kept me out of physical activity altogether. But as my junior year approached, I wanted to participate in at least one sport. My doctor and I agreed on track.

The first scheduled event of the year was the City-Wide Indoor Meet held in the field house at the University of Minnesota. Each of the eleven public high schools in Minneapolis was allowed to enter three participants per event. I placed third in the high jump from our school in the preliminaries and made the finals by the skin of my teeth.

In the week or so preceding the meet I practiced as precisely and thoroughly as I knew how. A friend from another high school taught me everything he knew about high jumping, and I did my best to learn the essentials of the event from him.

When the day of the meet came, I can remember wondering why I was even suited up. As the bar was elevated from 4' 10" on up, and as I cleared each increased height, my confidence seemed to build. Finally, with the help of a potent flow of adrenaline, I was the only one of thirty-three entrants to clear 5' 7" and became the Minneapolis city champion in the high jump.

I remember the look of surprise on the face of our coach. He was astonished, as I had previously shown no promise whatever. And I can still recall arriving at my father's grocery store, hugging him and telling him I had won the meet. I ran home, a half block away, and announced to my mother, "I'm city champ!"

Inside, I was a new person. My self-concept had changed. The luster of winning faded rapidly, but for once I had excelled in something. And even though I won other meets in the months that followed, that initial experience stayed with me. I knew that by national high school standards I was, at best, only average, but that didn't matter. In the local competition in which I was being rated, I was number one. I had tasted victory in one area of life, and I wanted to taste it again.

But it wasn't as easy as just *wanting* to. In college, on the basis of my high school accomplishments, I was admitted to what I felt was (and which was then considered "cool") a top fraternity. But social confidence never came easily for me. At fraternity meetings I would stand up to say something and promptly forget everything I had planned to express. I froze in the presence of people I felt were superior to me. Academically, I viewed myself as only mediocre, and thus was satisfied scholastically with the status quo.

Although becoming a Christian just before my twenty-first birthday changed many inner longings in my life, there still remained that fear of man. While I was counting on Jesus

13

Christ to take care of me in the life to come and to watch over me *generally* in this present life, it never dawned on me that I could draw upon His power for the *details* of right now. In short, I did not *expect* to be consistently victorious with Him. The thought of ever being an aggressive Christian— one who by faith appropriates the life of the overcoming Christ — did not occur to me. I wasn't necessarily a coward; I was simply ignorant of the full potential of Jesus Christ living in me.

I was still trying to put *myself* across. I assumed people were evaluating me as representing Jesus Christ, rather than encountering Jesus Christ as expressed in my life.

It has been twelve years since the Lord became a reality for me. Since that time it seems everything around me has changed (not that He has changed). He is the same, "yesterday, and today, and forever."[1] It is the *world* that has changed. Life is faster, bolder, more complicated, and more depressing. On a scale from zero to one hundred, temptation is way up, and there are new problems.

But, thank God, there are new solutions. No—let me take that back. Not really *new* solutions, but *new applications* for the ageless, permanent One.

Increasingly, it seems, those who are being drawn to Him are coming with a solidarity and a "statement of intent" that is far beyond the convenience and "acceptable standards" that have earmarked so many of us believers far too long. The Spirit of God is doing something new.

Just the other day, for example, the letter which follows came to my attention. It was written to a close friend, thanking him for pointing the young writer to Christ. It is written in the *lingua franca* of the "turned-on generation."

> Dear Jim:
> I just want to let you in on what's been happening since I last saw you. The Saturday before Thanksgiving I dumped the stuff . . . all of it! I was afraid to do it before I went home, but I just couldn't keep it up any longer.
> It was bad, but not as bad as I had envisioned. I guess everything is that way. You build it up in your mind until it reaches unreal proportions. I prayed, like I have never prayed before!

When it got real bad, I tripped out to Larry's. *Sometimes you have to rap*, and we rapped, and prayed, and in a few days I was through the physical tensions (time-bomb).

I went home and told my folks everything . . . I mean everything! I think it relieved them more than upset them. You see, they knew it, but just didn't know how to cope with it (or me). Anyway, I've seen Larry every day since I got back and I've been learning some heavy things. I think he has learned a few things, too, because I have been able to let him in on the drug scene from the other side of the wall. Maybe it will help him when he deals with it again, and he will. We learn from each other, all of us.

When I was home, I ran into a "friend" (connection) from school. I was in a department store, and he spotted me and was trying to let me in on the load. I know he didn't believe me when I told him I had kicked it. Anyway, I knew then that I was off the stuff.

Larry and I and a lot of other guys have been getting together (as a matter of fact, we hit it last night) and really getting with God. We're hitting the Book, too. It's all there!

There is no way I can thank you enough for showing me the crack in the door. It's open all the way now. I'm grooving on people, life, and God, especially God. I couldn't have done it alone.

If you run into any heads, tell them about me. And if they really want to break out, you can even give them my address. I'll be more than happy to write them. Sometimes you've got to see someone who has been through it.

Well, that's about it and thanks again.

Greg

SOMETIMES YOU HAVE TO RAP

What a document of freedom from a college student who has crammed more into his life than most of us will ever know, or even care to know.

It is a timeless principle of God, that where sin abounds, grace abounds all the more.[2] Jesus saw far greater response from those deeply involved in moral depravity than He did from those possessing self-awarded "goodness." "I have come to heal the sick," He said. "Those who are well do not need the services of a physician."[3]

This "sin scene" of today is, in one sense, a great source of encouragement. God says He uses even the wrath of men to praise Him.[4] The church was at an all-time low when the Reformation broke out. Two hundred years later England was morally bankrupt when along came the church renewal personified by John Wesley and those God used him to reach.

The current trend should prove no exception in provoking a hunger on the part of mankind for a deep, inner working of God the Holy Spirit. He has not abdicated His throne! And though the next awakening may come in the wake of widespread and even severe persecution of those who follow Christ, let us not think for a moment that God has fallen asleep and is not in the midst of bold workings in the hearts of men!

Sometimes you have to rap. You probably feel that way. I feel that way. I want to see some things brought out and exposed to the light of what the Lord Jesus Christ has to say and offer to this generation of seekers and sleepers—seekers among the throng of those who have never tasted of the goodness of His presence, and sleepers from among those who call Him Lord and yet have missed out on the thrill of responding to Him in the context of an "everyday life" basis.

In grad school one professor said that before you can bring people into the light, you must first dig a pit out of which they will seek to escape. Let's rap on the essence of the pit!

WAR

To be "in" today, you must have something to say on war and its opponent, peace. In a college dorm room not long ago, I spied a poster which read, "Suppose they gave a war and nobody showed up?"

I mention the subject of war not because there is something new to be said for or against it, but because a vast number of our fellow human beings—especially the younger ones—are all uptight over it. People are shook because it isn't moral.

Has there ever been a war that was moral? The issue, it seems, is not whether a war is *moral* but whether it is *popular*, so far as public opinion is concerned.

World War II was not moral, but it *was* popular. Today's war is not moral either, but the thing that brings dissent is that it is not popular. In the world, whether a thing is popular or not has nothing to to with its morality. Extramarital sex, for example, is extremely popular at this point in history. So are drug trips and marijuana parties. That does not say one thing, however, about their morality.

At UCLA recently I heard a student put forth an argument that we should depart from Southeast Asia on the basis of the Fifth Commandment. But at the same time, he was going to bed with his girl and felt no compulsion to bring a cessation to that activity because he felt it was "meaningful." Last year in America over 25,000 died in highway mishaps because the drivers were under the influence of alcohol. That was about six times more than the number of Americans killed in Viet Nam that same year.[5] "Why don't you demonstrate against motorists who drink?" came the question. There was no response.

In 1969 in New York City alone a reported fifty-five people (and no doubt a great number *not* reported) died from an overdose or misuse of drugs.[6] "Why don't you demonstrate against drugs?" came the question. There was no response.

We've been sold a fake line! We don't see the forest for the trees. Certainly killing is immoral. People on the forefront of what makes news in the world have said it strongly and said it well. But why do so many of the same cats who say war is immoral rely upon drugs to keep them going, which often results in blown minds and physical death? Doesn't that get to you — just a bit?

When something is popular, we try to find a rationale to make it moral. When something is unpopular, we look for ways to present it as being immoral. If it is both unpopular and immoral, like the war, the world uses God's standards to declare it immoral. But if it is popular and immoral, then a philosophic system is erected to make it *look* moral (like free sex or drug trips) because it can purportedly give you a closer insight into yourself, or some other such garbage. It is a pitiful mind which contends it is noble to say, "I want to go to bed with you because it's meaningful." By that same logic another misguided person could retort, "I want to kill you because it's meaningful."

Let's either groove with God or groove with the world. But let's bag this nonsense of keeping one foot in His kingdom and the other in the kingdom of this world by saying one thing and doing another. It is their insight into this inconsistency on the part of many "activists" which is serving as one of the reasons that many high school and college-age people are trusting in Christ today.

DRUGS

Though the matter of drugs has just been mentioned, let's hit it for a moment from a different angle: the *need* for drugs.

I sometimes think that if I were growing up as a member of this current generation, I'd want to trip out too. They really have hit the nail on the head in their analysis of this present world—there is little about it that holds any meaning.

"So let's escape." "Let's step out of reality."

But whoever said that in the world there is reality? If this present world is ultimate reality, count me out! I want no part of it. And the truth of God is that this is *not* reality. Reality is in Jesus Christ. "I am the Way and the Truth and the Life,"[7] He said. "You will know the truth and the truth will set you free."[8]

I can empathize with those who say they want to take a trip to escape, but a trip is a poor substitute for the real way out.

God is all for our coming out. If He had been against it, He would have withheld His Son, Jesus Christ, from coming into the world. He came *in* that we might come *out!* Jesus never promised escape from the physical world in this life, but He did tell us of a promised dominion over it. He said, "In the world you will have trouble; but have courage! I have overcome the world."[9]

It seems the presence of drugs as a quasi-solution to world pressure has awakened many to the need for an alternative to the best this present age can offer. If you can't find the answer inside the world, look outside, beyond. Drugs give a synthetic, temporary beyond; Jesus gives one that lasts.

18

THE BUSINESS WORLD

Contrary to the opinions of many youth, those who are out in the everyday world are beginning to see and say many of the same things. Over lunch recently a stockbroker friend relayed how carrying on business today is becoming next to impossible. "The records we are forced to keep are about to kill us," he said. "And it's getting worse each year. Sometimes I feel we have lost control of our surroundings." He went on to relate how friends in other kinds of business are sensing the same thing. The role of the individual and the possibility for his personal control of his environment seem to be lessening all the time. People find they are part of the system without even realizing how they got there!

A neighbor lady commented not long ago concerning a good friend of the family who had been a prominent business executive in a large city when, suddenly, he abandoned his position, bought a farm in a rural area, and became a policeman in a small secluded town. He was so happy he could not express it. Her own husband, she went on to say, had relinquished his chosen career, due to constant pressure and demands, and had taken a job pumping gas in a filling station. "We're having a real time adjusting to our new budget," she said, "but I'd still far rather live this way than to have him eaten alive by the business monster and rarely get to see the man. We've never been happier or more at ease."

Let's face it; the pressure is on. Is there a way to live above it?

THE HIPPIE CULT

A society within a society has come to the fore in this country. Many feel the hippies are a barnacle upon the world. Others feel they are part of an enlightened generation which has seen a ray of hope and moved on to something new and fresh.

Whatever the correct analysis of the culture, there are some reliable general observations which can be drawn. First, a seemingly huge percentage of the "freaks" are those who, by their own admission, not only couldn't cut it with the sharp, glistening white-teeth society, but didn't care to. They are those who couldn't or didn't make it in the world system.

Secondly, a great percentage of them are from homes of wealth and plenty. But so what? Where was the holding force of such an environment? Every other revolution in world history has been composed of the disenchanteds who discovered each other, and this one is no exception. Their influence in this country has been so strong that without press agents, public relations reps, or even group determination, they have influenced the music, dress, hair styles, theater, politics — and to a great extent the basic life-style — of an entire nation.

They came on at the right time.

But is there more to it than that? Has God some lessons for us from this phenomenon? And even if much of what they are purporting is true, will, in the next generation or two, child-products of this society "drop out" into another culture due to limitations, lack of understanding, tradition, or something else?

Thirdly, the young intelligentsia make up a large portion of this curious culture. They're not dummies. A reasoned rationale accompanies their departure from today. Far from lazy, they have simply turned their efforts elsewhere.

And you should see them when they turn to Christ! The healthiest believers, as a group, I have ever seen are converted hippies and freaks. They are less hung up on "things" than the vast majority of "regular" believers. Discipleship is not an issue for them. They just *want* to follow their King. But, of course, most continue without a knowledge of God.

RACISM

Many sociologists are expecting racism to be the eventual downfall of man. Not only have color barriers hindered tranquility in this country, but the problem is rampant the world over. India with her caste system and Africa with her tribalism and apartheid join in the racial strife that plagues the world. Historically, it is even fair to say that the current

Middle East Arab-Israeli conflict is basically racial in nature.

Racism in this country takes different forms. Having lived in several sections of America during the past ten years, I have made an observation which I believe generally holds true. In the North, the whites tend to accept the blacks as a race but have little contact or interaction with them as individuals. Many vocal advocates of civil rights yell their heads off for equality and then go back home again to their lily-white neighborhoods.

In the South, the mood has tended to be a friendly one between whites and blacks on the personal level but more cautious on the social level. You have people warm and friendly toward each other as individuals, but the white community stays aloof from the black. The tensions arising from both these situations are severe and without ready solution.

This is but a sample of the backdrop of today's world. Yet it is in this paranoid society that God chooses to work because it is here that people yearn for wholeness and restoration. The kingdom of God always seems to flourish in times of upheaval because the carnage of human failure provides such a stark and unmistakable contrast to the righteousness of God.

It is this kingdom of God which is our alternative—both in its current form as expressed through the body of Christ, and in its ultimate, eternal form in our union forever with Jesus Christ. Our new identity, then, is neither "giving up" our human kingdoms nor "doing" things appropriate to His kingdom; our new identity is allowing Christ to produce His life within us. I trust we will become so completely captivated by our Great King that saying farewell to stale human life will be the most natural course that we could possibly take.

A Quiet Surge of Force

I will break down this temple made by hands
and in three days build another
made without hands.

— Jesus of Nazareth

2

A Quiet Surge of Force

God is quietly counteracting today's mad scene with a movement all His own. People are beginning to sense that something new and different is happening. I just received a letter from the editor of a well-known magazine whose purpose it is to set forth the workings of the Spirit of God in this day and age. "I've never said this before in twenty years," he wrote, "but I really believe that Jesus Christ will come back any day."

It is apparent throughout the New Testament that the re-entry of Jesus Christ into history as Lord of lords and King of kings will be preceded by a new awakening within His Church. True, it is predicted that when He comes He will not find faith on the earth.[1] But He is not referring to those who are following Him and expectantly awaiting His kingdom. He is talking generally about the inhabitants of the physical earth.

God has much to say about the Church, the people of God, being prepared as a bride to meet the Bridegroom.[2] And it is this preparation — a making ready — that we seem so clearly to be experiencing now.

A few years ago I was quite alarmed at the reports I was hearing of the hippie cults on the West Coast. Here, it seemed, was a segment of society abandoned by God and sophisticated man. But a subsequent trip (or should I say "journey!") to the Coast revealed another side to the story. What we had heard about the decadent values and nihilistic philosophies of many within these groups was true. In some cases I felt the actual life-style of these people was worse than published reports.

But God was at work, too.

I recall meeting one group of "Christian hippies"—many, former acid heads—whom I shall never forget. They were centered just north of San Diego. Somehow, about fifty of them had responded to Christ and had come into a fresh and living relationship with Him. As they described how the Spirit of God had worked in their midst, little mention was made of human instruments or the efforts of other men to reach them with the message. They described it as something that God alone was doing in His sovereign majesty.

This particular group of young men and women began attending an organized church in the area where the pastor was adept at communicating the Word of God in understandable and meaningful terms. (It should be noted that most of these people continued to dress as they had prior to their conversion. As I talked with them, they said they had retained this mode of dress to more easily identify with others of their group who did not know Christ.)

The first few Sundays their visits to the church worked out fine. After a month or so, however, problems began to arise. Many in the church felt that the presence of this large group of—in their eyes—non-conformists would tend to scare off the "straights." The elders became concerned over the outward appearance of these people and the effect it might have on others in the community who might wish to come and hear the Word of God but would be hesitant to do so because of the apparent conflict of values. After a hasty board meeting, the "Christian hippies" related, they were asked to sit in the balcony.

That worked for about two weeks. It became obvious, however, that the situation would be best solved by the departure of these new believers. (This is not to say that those within the institutional church responded unnaturally or even wrongly. They, no doubt, were thinking in terms of the total community and not just that small segment of people. The question *does* come, however, that if the Holy Spirit is working on a wide scale to draw all breeds of humanity to the Father, can the organized church as we know it relax and modify its human standards to receive these new believers? Or is God going to simply move outside and continue His work in new surroundings?)

The end result of this whole dilemma was that the "flower children" felt the best thing in God's sight—for their own good and the good of others—was to leave the structured assembly and worship the Lord Jesus on their own.

They began meeting on the beach, singing, praying, and asking God to do new and mighty things. Many people came to Christ as a result. I met with several of those involved in this new manifestation of God's activity. It was nothing weird—being around them was not at all uncomfortable. They were thrilled over their new life, and what they had was *real*. Christ was most visible in their midst. And the fact that they chose to stay outside the gates benefited all concerned.

The "Jesus Movement," as the news media refer to is, is gaining tremendous momentum. And it's not just long-hairs. Kids from all types of backgrounds are meeting together in homes, parks, college student unions to give praise to the Lord and encouragement to each other. They are *alive* in Jesus Christ.

This type of thing—this new happening of the Holy Spirit—is more and more prominent on many fronts. With the tremendous outpouring of the kingdom of darkness in all its manifestations, something far more powerful than "church tradition" or institutional loyalty will be needed to bare the Arm of God. As good as sincere Christian effort may be when it is compared to the anemia of worldliness, *nothing* apart from the divine working of the Holy Spirit, in all power and dominion, is good enough to forge ahead of and lay ruin the kingdom of this world!

In First Kings 6:7 God says, "The house was built of stones dressed at the quarry; there was no sound of hammer, chisel, or any other iron tool while the house was being built." The description in this passage is of the beginning efforts to erect Solomon's Temple. You will notice that the edifice was constructed without the sound of ax or hammer.

When God does something, *noise is not necessary!* There is no need for bright lights and glaring marquee. Neither must men receive the credit. The desire of our Father is to perform a work in this (as any) age that is so solid, miraculous, and lasting that no man could possibly receive the glory.

I must confess at this point that I really wonder if we as believers are ready for a *widespread* working of the Spirit of God. So many of our efforts are channeled through visible means. God is planning something deeper. I am not in any way contending that God cannot or will not do something which is visible. The problem is that we are so prone to *promote* it! If some people receive Christ through the particular institution with which we are working, that is such great material for our monthly news report. It encourages others to give financially and to get involved. But as pure as our own motives may be simply to enhance and build the momentum of the Spirit's working, we are, in effect, saying that *we* did it.

Never before in history has there been such great opportunity to spread the message of Jesus Christ. We have radio, television, the printed page, films, and even computers as communications media. And still, we are told, the proclamation of the Good News is not keeping abreast of the expansion in population. In the first century none of the above was available. There was only the Holy Spirit leading and instructing the Church. That is not to say we should scrap the methods of communication we have available today. It is to say, however, that apart from trusting the Holy Spirit, all of our efforts are in vain.

In Ephesians 2:19-22 we have the positive description of how the Holy Spirit performs His work.

19. Therefore, you are no longer strangers and immigrants, but you are fellow citizens with the saints and members of God's household;

20. you are constructed on the foundation of the apostles and prophets, of which the cornerstone is Christ Jesus.

21. The whole building, framed together in Him, rises into a temple that is holy in the Lord,

22. in whom you also are built up together for a dwelling of God in the Spirit.

It's exactly the same principle which we found in the passage in First Kings. As a matter of fact, I believe Paul is refering directly to that Old Testament reference as he describes the building of the spiritual temple of God. There's no noise here either!

If you are in the fellowship of Jesus Christ, you are being built up in Him. What a tremendous consolation. God has not left you on your own. You are part of an unstructured structure, an unprogrammed program of believers. You are *necessary*. With God, every unit of construction counts. He is fitting or molding us to be placed together with the other constructive elements. And to top it all off, God promises to dwell in the midst of us through the Holy Spirit.

Can you think of anything more exciting or adventuresome than being chosen by God to be, along with countless other brothers and sisters, the object of His habitation? In Christ there is *no* place for human isolation or estrangement. We are being built up *together!* We, as His followers, are *one*.

The "New J"

There is a river whose streams
make glad the city of God,
the holy dwelling of the Most High.

— David

3

The "New J"

The plan of God for us is not merely to build us into a dwelling for His Spirit on this earth and leave it at that. His plan encompasses a magnitude of life which our natural minds could never see and which even our enlivened spirits can scarcely comprehend!

In the last two chapters of the book of Revelation God gives us a picture, through the eyes of the apostle John, of what lies ahead. This passage is significant for several reasons.

First, it shows the final goal of God's purpose for us. In other words God is not working within our lives just to give us "abundant life" here on earth. He is working within us as individuals and as the body of Christ to make us ready for His eternal plan.

Secondly, these chapters show us what spiritual life is *really* like because those old enemies "sin" and "death" no longer exist. They have both been sealed up together in the doom predetermined for them before the ages began. Thus we see the beauty of the Kingdom of God in all its fullness and majesty.

Thirdly, in allowing the Holy Spirit to apply these truths to our understanding, we are enabled to see the "big picture on the wide screen" and understand more fully the overall plan and purpose of God. It has been said that a person having no grip on eternity has no hold in time. If we can but see where we are headed, we can far better comprehend the why and the wherefore of what God is seeking to do within us at this present hour.

To give some orientation to this passage, let me compare it with marriage. In human terms, we have the courtship or engagement, the marriage ceremony itself, the honeymoon, and the life together which follows.

For the sake of illustration let us compare the courtship and engagement period with our spiritual lives right now. We are, as it were, engaged to be married to the Lord Jesus. The Scriptures call us His bride. Soon (and I personally believe really soon!) there will be the wedding ceremony, where we as His bride are joined to Him forever. John, the apostle, speaks in this context in Revelation of the joining together and the marriage supper of the Lamb which is to occur when believers are taken to be with Him.[1]

The honeymoon can be compared to the millennial reign with Christ—the initial period of one thousand years when, after being joined with Him, we reign with Him on earth.[2] Finally, after the last enemy, death, has been subdued,[3] we shall live and rule with Him in a life which never ends. It is this last "married life" era with which we are concerning ourselves here.

THE CITY OF GOD

Writing in approximately A.D. 90, the apostle John was thrust into the future by the Spirit of God and shown most vividly a City that is to come.

1. Then I saw a new heaven and a new earth; for the first heaven and the first earth had passed away, and no longer was there any sea.

2. I also saw the holy city, the new Jerusalem, descending out of heaven from God, and made ready as a bride adorned for her husband.

3. And I heard a loud voice from the throne say, "Behold, God's dwelling place is among men, and He will dwell with them; they shall be His people, and God Himself will be with them

4. and shall wipe away every tear from their eyes. Death shall be no longer, nor mourning, nor crying, nor any further pain, because the former things have passed away."

(Revelation 21:1-4)

Throughout history God has promised a city to the Jews. Abraham was evidently the first to hear of it, and we are told he spent a good portion of his life in expectation of a city "whose Architect and Builder is God."[4] David wrote of the city and told of his eagerness to move in and get settled.[5] Isaiah wrote of the revelation of this grand new place of life and spoke most enthusiastically of its glory.[6] And when we believe in Jesus Christ and are grafted into believing Israel,[7] we are co-recipients of these same promises and fellow-heirs of the kingdom of God!

Remember when Jesus said that His Father's house had many mansions and that He was going to prepare a place for us and then come back for us so that we could move in there with Him?[8]

What John is describing here is just what Jesus left this planet to prepare. In fact He is probably working on it right now to complete the finishing touches in time for the Father to send Him back for us. And as you read through the closing two chapters of Revelation, you will appreciate this promise from the Lord even more.

In verse three we read that God will literally dwell among us. That's good news for the Gentile believer, but it's incredible news for the Jew who believes. In the Old Testament, God was rarely so intimate with men. He dwelt in the Holy of

Holies in the Tabernacle and only Israel's high priest ever went into that chamber, and then only once each year.[9] For those of us who know Christ in this age of grace, the Holy Spirit brings the life of Christ within us and manifests His presence in a reality that is true but invisible.

Here, however, God is promising that He will dwell with His sons and daughters face to face. What a thrill to live in His city with Him, to reign in power and holiness.

In verse four God promises total liberation from all that deceives and terrifies us today. Death, crying, and pain are gone, and *all* the former things go by the boards—no more social pressures, taxes, funerals, hurts, let downs, final exams, or struggles to succeed. And the more I see this, the more I yearn to be there *now*.

And I can. So can you. In Christ we are already seated in the heavenlies![10] If we but see the citizenship which is presently ours, we will know what reality is in Jesus and that we are with Him this moment at God's right hand. If we through the Holy Spirit can see our destined citizenship as, eternally speaking, *already* here, life on this planet becomes merely a sideshow that will soon move on. Or to say it another way, when we are born of the Spirit, we are placed at His right hand to experience kingdom life in our spirits before it is ever revealed. That means today—right now. And there is *nothing* like it!

John goes on to say that God will make all things new. The promise is that we will drink freely of the water of life. Though this is a definite reference to what lies ahead, nonetheless this water is available to us now. It is the same water Jesus promised the woman at the well in John 4. As we shall be thoroughly satisfied by Him in the city of our God, so shall we experience the quenching of our thirst if we choose to drink of the water of life here and now.

The antithesis to the New Jerusalem is described in Revelation 21:8 as a burning lake. Those whose works reveal a life estranged from God will receive this gruesome inheritance. Most of the adjectives in that verse—unbelieving, depraved, murdering, immoral—describe people who traditionally have known they are living apart from Jesus Christ.

But there is one group of individuals mentioned who are often so totally deceived by Satan that they are virtually unaware of what they are involved in. I'm speaking of those who practice the magic arts. There is a tremendous revival today in this manifestation of spiritual death, and its mention in this passage gives clear and ample warning of the dangers involved. When God says that the magic art bit—that is, witchcraft, drug trips, Satan worship, astrology, etc. (see Deuteronomy 18:9-12)—is a bummer, *please* take His word for it! This stuff is the way of death. If you happen to be involved with this scene or are considering experimenting with it, shake it off and take notice: God says it will end in the pit. Sorcery is the game the antichrist plays to lure people to share his destiny in the lake of fire.

The City of God houses the wife of the Lamb. In fact, look at the description John gives in 21:9-11, " 'Come this way. I will show you the bride, the Lamb's wife.' He then conveyed me in the Spirit to a great and lofty mountain and showed me Jerusalem, the holy city, coming down out of heaven from God with the glory of God." The implication is that the "bride" and the "City" are really one. Therefore, as our spirits are one with Christ in time, we continue on as one with Him in eternity. We are being built up right now into that which we are becoming — the bride of Christ, the City of God.

Do you see it? This is not mere rhetoric. God has a reason for our belonging to Him far above simply being "good" in this present life. He is molding us as stones to compose the structure of which He alone is Builder and Architect. Every move He makes in our lives today has purpose and meaning that is eternal. When Jerusalem descends from heaven, those who belong to Christ will move right in. God is working in us and through us ahead of time to prepare us for that event which lasts forever!

The physical description of the City is beyond comparison. It has twelve gates and twelve foundation stones, each made of a rare and precious mineral. It is cube-shaped, each side measuring 1500 miles, like a huge condominium with its inhabitants filling the entire structure.[11] And look at the magnificent center court:

22. I saw no temple in it, for the Lord God Omnipotent is its temple, and so is the Lamb.

23. The city has no need of the sun or of the moon to shine on it, because God's glory illumines it and the Lamb is its light.

24. By its light the nations will walk and to it the kings of the earth will bring their splendor.

25. Its gates shall not at all be closed during the day, for there will be no night there.

26. Into it they will carry the glory and the honor of the nations.

27. But nothing unclean nor anyone practicing immorality and falsehood shall ever enter it, but only those whose names have been recorded in the Lamb's Book of Life.

(Revelation 21:22-27)

The action central of the City of God is Jesus Christ Himself. He is its temple and its throne, and it is He who lights the city so completely that night is gone forever. Only the splendor of daylight will be known to those who live there.

THE RESTORATION OF LIFE

As chapter twenty-two of Revelation opens, you will notice something that to me is amazing. It is almost a re-enactment of the first two chapters of Genesis. The river is there, the tree of life reappears, and God and man are reunited. It is as though the Lord has been working with man ever since he fell to bring him back to that relationship with Himself that existed in paradise.

1. He then showed me the river of the water of life, as clear as crystal, flowing forth from the throne of God and of the Lamb,

2. and running through the middle of the street, and on this side and that side of the river, the tree of life, bearing twelve kinds of fruit, yielding its fruit every month. And the leaves of the tree are for the healing of the nations.

(Revelation 22:1,2)

This is what Paul calls God's "eternal purpose" in Ephesians 3:11. Through the centuries He has been bringing man back to Himself and preparing him for His Kingdom. And our Lord and Savior Jesus Christ has been, is, and will be the source of that life which reconciles us to the Father and the Father to us.

God's last word of Biblical revelation to man concerned the nature of our everlasting relationship with Him and with each other. We are being molded now to join Him there. " . . . and they shall reign forever and ever."[12]

Farewell to the Fake I.D.

Therefore, dear friends, since you have these expectations, do your utmost to be found at peace with Him— spotless and blameless.

— Simon Peter

4

Farewell to the Fake I.D.

When I first began to understand my (our) life ahead with Jesus Christ as being something specific and definable, it changed my whole view of things. First, it made a myriad of truths which I had previously learned suddenly fit into place. I'll describe how this happened in the remaining chapters of this book. Secondly, I discovered new attitudes came as a result of seeing my destiny. I wish to relate these in this chapter.

A WHOLE NEW PURPOSE FOR LIVING

When you start to understand eternity, life right then suddenly becomes a much bigger deal. You see what happens earthside really *is* in God's plan — He is engaged in the outworking of a total purpose in which your life is involved.

I think many times we feel that an event or an experience is "here today and gone tomorrow," and that's it. But for the believer there is much more to it than that. When we see the City of God and our personal heritage there, we start living in the light of eternity rather than only in the light of time.

A LIFE THAT REIGNS

I must confess that I used to be somewhat hesitant to leave this earth and go on to what I nebulously called heaven. All I ever envisioned was inactivity, choirs, and harps. Nothing wrong with good music, but not *just* that for all eternity.

John said he *saw* the holy city descending down out of heaven from God.[1] And through his eyes, my spirit can say with him that I see the City and my identity is truly there. And by the promise of God I see myself as a part of that City, *living and reigning* with Him and the rest of my fellow citizens. I see a tremendously active life — active as God is active. It's no longer nebulous. It's seeable, touchable, locatable. There is still much to understand and comprehend — I'll just have to wait to get there before I see it as God does. But it's as though He has let me partake of a portion of this setting in my spirit to let me know it's there.

When we moved to Memphis, Tennessee, a couple of years ago, we felt sure we'd like it because we had previously seen the town. We liked the homes, the parks, and the way of life. Most importantly, we liked the people whom we met on our initial visit. They seemed like the kind of folks with whom we would enjoy associating.

Now that we have lived here awhile, we *know* we like it. We have made some wonderful friends and our new brothers and sisters in Christ are just great. We are now experiencing that which, prior to our making the move, we had only a glimpse.

This is but a minute fraction of the way I feel about my up and coming move into the New Jerusalem. I like so much of what I see from a great distance. I like its beauty, its life of reign, its citizens, and most of all, its great King!

SO WHAT ABOUT NOW?

To transfer the anticipation of city life to "country life"

(life on earth) is something that the Holy Spirit must do within us. This is more than just the proverbial "pie in the sky." When we see our lives as eternally planted *there*, and our lives now as but a brief prologue, at best, to what lies ahead, certain things will almost inevitably occur within us.

Part of what I see for me right now is "reigning training." God is using the circumstances of this earthly life to equip me as a person, and His Bride as a multiplicity of persons-made-one, to prepare us for living forever with Him. He sometimes tries our faith to make us patient; He allows us weakness to make us strong; He lets us stumble to teach us to stand; He buoys us up to encourage us to offer praise.

Let me try some gut-level specifics. Could it be you have failed in business (if you have) to help make you ready to meet Him? Has He given you rampant success to help show you its meaninglessness apart from a walk with Him, or perhaps to allow you a stepping stone to give of yourself to others in the way an average person never could? Has He taken a child from you, or a lover or a friend, to teach *you* to be *His* child or His lover or His friend? Does He allow your absolute fatigue from the rat race of daily life to make you cry out "why?" and thereby learn from Him a new level of trust and dependence upon the Lord Jesus?

I cannot answer these questions for you. Sometimes I have a most difficult time answering them for myself! But we may rest in this: God is at work mightily within us both to will and do of His good pleasure.[2] He is preparing us for city living.

Something else I am beginning to see is that in taking up residence now in the City of God, I understand far better how I feel about this present world and how I fit into it.

In Hebrews chapter eleven we see how the promise of the City affected Abraham. As you read the passages which follow, remember that Abraham lived in a period of history in which life was strikingly more simple than it is today.

8. By faith Abraham obeyed when he was called to go out to a place which he was to receive for an inheritance, and he migrated without any idea where he was going.
9. By faith he lived in the land of promise as in a foreign

country, living in tents, as did Isaac and Jacob who were joint heirs with him of the same promise.

10. For he was looking for the city with foundations, whose Architect and Builder is God.

13. These all died in faith without having received what was promised them, but they saw it from a distance and welcomed it, confessing that they were foreigners and exiles on the earth.

14. For those who say such things make it plain that they are looking for a homeland,

15. and if they had in mind that country from which they went out, they would have had a chance to return.

16. But now they are longing for a better, that is, a heavenly country; accordingly, God is not ashamed of being called their God. In fact, He has prepared a city for them. (Hebrews 11:8-10, 13-16).

Abraham, the father of Israel, was wandering around the backside of the desert in 2500 B.C. looking for the same city that we are looking for today. And notice how he responded. He saw himself as a foreigner and exile on the earth! Wow — what a privilege to see that truth now, rather than to have to admit it later. He had a chance to return to his old, world-centered (country) life, but he chose instead to take up current residence in the heavenlies (city life) where his true identity lay.

The joy of being freed *now* from the enchantment of the world system is fantastic! I used to hear sermons on "forsaking the world," "coming apart and being separate," and "giving up worldliness," but they never seemed to click. Now it's no longer the issue. When I see God's promise of a city prepared for me, an everlasting place to live, attitudes concerning the world seem to take care of themselves. Do you identify with that?

I spend five days a week in the business world as a money-raiser for a large metropolitan state university, and I find my job and the people with whom I work most enjoyable. I'm where the Lord wants me. Sometimes I come home mentally beat. Other times pressures are minimal. Occasionally I seriously (and I am not even remotely kidding) consider moving to the country and completely bagging it all — just to raise crops, animals, and kids. But the Lord gives no peace. So I am learning — learning to fit into the world, to give myself honestly and sincerely to my work, my superiors, and colleagues. I am able to say "thank you" for the opportunity of working.

But though I am fitting in, I am different. Do you sense that about yourself?

If you are a housewife, or a 40-hour-per-week breadwinner, or a kid who goes to school, do you know what I am trying to say? You're in it, but not of it.

I see other people in our town who work just as hard as I do, but who are identified with country life in a way I no longer am. Our production records look about the same, but our attitudes are different. To them (and I am saying this as best I can with a heart that does not wish to condemn) being a success is really a super deal. It means getting ahead and moving up the ladder. For me, that's no longer where it's at. And that is not because I am *trying not* to be attached to getting ahead. It is because I see in looking beyond to the house of the Lord, and looking now to the body or people of the Lord, that this "country climbing" just doesn't get it. Sure I work hard. But I see a life far above raises and success and goal-setting that intrigues me so much that my identity has become other-worldly rather than worldly. "For to me to live is Christ and to die is gain."[3] What more can I say?

Our godly forerunner David was taken up with the anticipation of the city of God. In Psalms 46 and 48, to which I referred earlier, he makes his feelings known. Rather than to quote from these and make personal comment on them, I suggest you read them for yourself and allow the Spirit of God to apply them to your own experience. Also read Isaiah 60-62, which reflects that prophet's joy as he looks ahead to the city of God.

When we grasp the phenomenal inheritance which God has prepared for us we become content to receive whatever the Lord chooses to give or withhold in this life. We see this present life as temporary and fleeting. Our brothers and sisters in Christ become eternal friends and everlasting members of the body of Jesus Christ. Division and strife seem so useless. The Church of God falls into perspective as being the most important treasure we can know on this earth. His Church is really His City projected down into time. In Him and His people we find our identity and reality.

We are released from this world to possess authority over it, not in a crassly dictatorial way, but in godly power and love. We are promised that whatever we bind on earth shall be bound in heaven,[4] and we have dominion over the earth.[5]

In the pages which remain I want to disclose to you the riches I have found in availing myself of the promises of God in light of my lasting inheritance. For me, the backdrop of overcoming the world has been to gaze with enchantment at Christ and His Kingdom and to know with assurance that I do not choose to return to the country from which I have come.

For we have here no permanent city![6]

God Is Right-Handed

Thy right hand, O Lord, is glorified in power.
— A Song of Israel

5

God Is Right-Handed

I once heard a story (supposedly true) of a man who moved west searching for silver. He built a small shack and lived for years on a shoestring, constantly looking for a new deposit of the valuable mineral which he sought.

After years of unsuccessful searching, he died. To everyone's surprise, as men were digging his grave, they discovered the huge vein of silver for which he had looked—and it ran right beneath his shack!

What an appropriate application that story possesses for many of us who believe in Jesus Christ! We know we need the riches that He offers freely to us, but we fail to see that He has *already* given us "all things that pertain unto life and godliness."[1] We just don't give our *experience* the chance to catch up with our current ledger of *possessions* which are ours by virtue of the fact that Jesus lives within us, and that we live in Him.

Prior to our coming to believe in Jesus Christ, we lived our lives in the only way natural humanity can live—by human resources. Since our spirits were dead, we had only our bodies and our minds with which to navigate in the world.

Or, broken down still further, we operated by our five senses. Many of us learned to really "groove" on the natural level. We operated quite effectively in the power of the flesh. We learned to manipulate people to get what we wanted. We found out how to talk our way into dominating situations we desired to control. Or, if we were more introverted, we just kept our mouths shut and rode with the tide. In any case we learned to live and move in the earthly realm. We did what we wanted and acted according to our own desires and for our own satisfaction.

In response to the kindness of God we began to follow Jesus Christ. But we had lived so long by sight that we had a tough time learning to walk by faith. We had lived in the arena of the body and the mind only and knew nothing of the Spirit of God—nor that He could be wedded to the human spirit. We were limited by those five senses.

And after years of claiming to know and walk with Jesus Christ, huge numbers of us still live and move in the energy of the flesh because we do not know there is another alternative available. Sure, we know we are "saved" and that if we were to die we would enter God's presence. But for some reason we miss out on the opportunity of living by the life of the Spirit here and now. We categorize our relationship with Christ to be only what He *will* do for us and what He *has* done for us, not what He *is* doing for us. Somehow we think that we will live in this world on our own and in the next by the power of God. We wouldn't say this, but isn't it really the way most of us live?

There are two bases of identity available to man: the one given by Adam and the one offered by Christ. We can either exist in the limitations of the fallen race or move on into the infinite possibilities of the walk in the Spirit. The world, as such, remains constant. The variable is in how we face the world: in the Adamic, fleshly way, or in the power and authority of the Holy Spirit.

I look forward to the day when we shall be stripped of the flesh and shall walk with the Lord in that "glorified body."[2] But until that happens, there has been tremendous provision made for us to navigate in this present world. More than 160 times in the New Testament Paul says that we as believers are "in Christ." If we are in Christ, the question naturally comes, "where *is* Jesus Christ?"

To be in Him means to be a part of Him. We are bone of His bone and flesh of His flesh,[3] one with Him. And right this moment Jesus Christ is seated at the magnificent place of authority and power over all the universe: the right hand of God.[4]

Throughout the Old and New Testaments the right hand of God is constantly described as the control center for His rule and domain. For example, we read:

> Exodus 15:6—Thy right hand, O Lord, is glorified in power; Thy right hand, O Lord, shattered the foe.

> Psalm 17:7 — In a marvelous way show Thine unfailing love, O Thou, who savest those who look for refuge from their adversaries at Thy right hand.

> Psalm 20:6—Now I know that the Lord saves His anointed; He answers him from His holy heaven with the saving might of His right hand.

> Psalm 48:10—In agreement with Thy name, O God, so is Thy praise to the ends of the earth; Thy right hand is full of Thy righteousness.

> Psalm 89:13—Thine is an arm with might; strong is Thy hand and high Thy right hand.

> Psalm 118:16—The right hand of the Lord is lifted up; the right hand of the Lord does valiantly.

> Matthew 22:44—The Lord said to my Lord, Sit at My right hand until I put Thy enemies under Thy feet.

The book of Hebrews tells us that when His work of redemption was finished, Jesus took His place at the right hand of His Father.[5] Paul says we are risen *with* Him![6] Sure, someday we shall join Him there face to face, but God wants us to see that we are present there with Him right now.

Remember the TV show many, many seasons back, when a deep voice would come through an echo chamber and say slowly and deliberately, "Y-o-u A-r-e T-h-e-r-e." The viewers would then go on a filmed trip of some out-of-the-way spot or event on the earth. It was make-believe.

But when God in His Word says, "You Are There," you are! Look carefully at Ephesians 1:17-23:

17. that the God of our Lord Jesus Christ, the glorious Father, might grant you a spirit of wisdom and of revelation for an understanding of Himself,

18. granting you eyes of the heart, so that you may know the nature of the hope to which you are called, and what is the wealth of His glorious inheritance in the saints,

19. and how overwhelmingly great is His power for us believers. It is like the working of His mighty strength,

20. which He exerted when He raised Christ from the dead and seated Him in the heavenly spheres at His right hand,

21. high above all government and authority, power and lordship, and every name that is named, not only in this but also in the future world.

22. God has placed everything under His feet and has given Him as head over everything for the church,

23. which is His body, the completeness of Him who fills the universe at all points.

Have you ever read anything better than that? The Lord Jesus this instant is seated *in your behalf* at the place of ultimate authority in all the universe—the right hand of God. Not only is this a place of honor and glory for *Him*, but He is exhibiting overwhelming power for *us* who are believers. God did this for a special purpose, for "in Christ Jesus He caused us to rise, and seated us with Him in the heavenly spheres, so that He might show in the future ages the immeasurable wealth of His grace, by means of His goodness to us through Christ Jesus" (Ephesians 2:6,7). He wants to show everyone His tremendous grace by how good He is to us. That really turns me on!

As we see ourselves in Christ, things begin to happen. Philippians 4:13 comes true as it talks about Jesus Christ "who keeps on pouring power into me." When we see ourselves elevated far above the daily drag of earth life and moved into the realm of the heavenlies, we experience God's power to overcome.

There is something to which I keep coming back. It is not as though the Lord has taken a bunch of individuals and raised them separately to identity in Him at God's right hand. He is talking here about the entire body of Christ; we are one together at His Throne! And because we are a unit there, we are a unit here. Can you see the body of Christ as God sees it—as one? (He has a better view of it than we do because He sees us there at His right hand.)

As we, in the Spirit, look through God's eyes at ourselves, we can see ourselves by His promissory Word as absolutely one. And if I see *us* as risen, I can see *me* as risen.

The power of God, then, is unrestrictedly available to those who belong to His Son. And as a member of Christ's body, I share in this power and authority. But do I dare utilize this megaton of strength on my own? It would scare me to death! In being one with other members of Christ, though, I not only better perceive this authority but am in harmony with those who mutually share it with me.

Knowing that I, as a member of Christ, have been raised to a new level of living, I begin to see that *God wants us to be what we have already become!* From an eternal viewpoint the Father sees all things reconciled in His Son. He sees us as seated with Christ in heavenly places. If someone were to ask God, "Where are all the believers?", most likely His response would be, "Here at my right hand, of course!"

The magnitude of this truth grips me with intensity, expectation, and joy. In Christ I am a conqueror! I can experience the same quality of life here and now as the Lord Jesus did during His stay on this earth. For though He came from the Father, He did not "use" His heritage of deity to "pull rank." He lived His life as a man—a person just like you and me—given over to the Holy Spirit. He lived as a *man* and relied upon the Father just as He asks that we do. Though He was the begotten Son of God, He lived as Son of Man, enduring and overcoming all the frustrations and deceptions which we face today.

He said, "No," with power to Satan; I can say, "No," to Satan.

He commanded miracles to the glory of God; I can see miracles to the glory of God.

He entered death; I enter death with Him, and sin has no dominion over one who is dead. I have died with Him—I am crucified with Him—and sin and death have no controlling power over me. This is a truth of the Spirit of God understood only through faith. "Constantly knowing this: our old self (me B.C.) was crucified so that the body of sin is powerless and we should no longer keep on being slaves to sin."[7] Our assets in Christ are such that we do not need to yield to sin.

Jesus was resurrected from the dead: We are raised to newness of life in Him. Jesus said, "Because I live, ye shall live also."[8] In time, that infusion of life will take place at the resurrection of all who believe. In God's sight we are alive from the dead *already* in Him. The Holy Spirit is pure, holy life living through us. We accept this as truth because God said it is true. To walk by faith is to walk by the life of the Holy Spirit. We perceive earth life through our five senses; He manifests God's life to those who believe Him through faith.

This is exactly Paul's point in Galatians: "I have been crucified with Christ and yet I live; it is no longer I who am living, however, but Christ keeps on living in me. The life I now live in the flesh I keep on living by the faith of the Son of God who loved me and gave Himself up for me."[9]

At this present hour, Christ sits in triumph at the right hand of the throne of God and so do we! It is here that Paul said the eyes of our understanding need to be opened. I cannot see myself as in Christ at God's right hand except by faith. But it is simple: God says I am there, so I am. My five senses say I am here, but my spirit witnesses that I am there. Since the Lord is truth, I take His word for it! As the body of Christ, we occupy the place of supreme power.

In a city in Mexico rush-hour traffic is directed by a policeman who stands on a pedestal in the middle of the intersection where he can be seen clearly. When he holds up his hand to motion a "stop," many tons of automotive power come abruptly to a halt. No one questions his authority, for the governing power of Mexico stands behind the man on that pedestal who motions to the traffic to stop or go.

One afternoon a tourist in the city pulled over to the side of the street near the busy intersection and asked the policeman directing the traffic to give him directions. The officer stepped down from the platform to come to the aid of the confused motorist.

Two little boys playing near the busy corner saw that the pedestal had become abandoned, and one of them made his way decisively through the traffic to perch himself atop the platform. Suddenly, he raised his hand and signaled for the automobiles to come to a stop. Scores of cars ground to a halt. They did not look to see who was giving directions; they stopped because someone in the place of authority had commanded them to stop.

So it is with the believer in Jesus Christ. As we take hold of the authority which has been delivered to us, we shall find ourselves possessing the same gracious power of life known by the Lord Jesus Himself. Power over sin; dominion over the circumstances surrounding us; and authority over impediments that emerge to withstand the might of the Kingdom of God.

Maybe for you it is something small: worry, insecurity, sophistication, hesitancy to be free.

Or something big: temptation, lack of faith, absence of power to overcome.

We are *in Christ*. And He wants us to reign with Him now in victory and power over the world, over the adversary, and over the fleshly limitations with which we are encased. God wants us to break away in Christ and to experience life with Him from on high.

It is here that Paul's exhortation to the Colossians takes on such vivid meaning:

1. If, then, you have been raised with Christ, seek the things which are above, where Christ is seated at God's right hand.

2. Apply your mind to things above, not to things on earth;

3. for you have died, and your life is hidden with Christ in God.

4. When Christ, who is our life, makes His appearance, then we also will appear in glory with Him.

(Colossians 3:1-4)

Let us not only *be* there, let us also *live* there. The identity and definition of our lives right now can only be seen as we acknowledge ourselves to be seated at the right hand of God. Seeing that we are citizens of a far better place than we know on this earth, let us rely instead on the life of Jesus Christ, coming forth in power from the matchless throne of God.

The Lame Duck

Resist the devil and he will flee from you.
—James

6

The Lame Duck

Perhaps the first glimpse I had of my authority in Jesus Christ over the dilemmas of human life was in understanding the fact that Satan was defeated at the Cross. For my first few years as a believer, I looked upon spiritual setbacks as strictly a matter of calculated inevitability—they were just bound to happen. But what God has for us as His children is far better than that.

Politically, a "lame duck" is the term attributed to an elected official, generally the President, when he fails in his bid for reelection to office in November, but does not actually leave that office until January 20th. Satan is a "lame duck." He was defeated in his effort to retain power at the Cross; he will be removed from office permanently just before the Kingdom of God is established. Currently, however, he is stripped of his authority over believers. Not stripped of his *activity*, but of his *authority*. There is no reason in the world why we who name the name of Jesus as Lord need to log time under Satan's deception. From God's point of view, Satan has been overcome by the Lord Jesus, and though Satan is still active in the world, God's promise is that he cannot touch us![1]

But let us clear the air as we begin in this chapter to consider the person and activities of Satan. He is no legend! We quip about his reality and his influence. I laugh myself sick when Flip Wilson gets on nationwide TV and says, "De ol' devil made me say dat!"—in the way only Flip Wilson can. It seems so typical—*typical* of the practical feelings of most all of us.

But Satan is no joke. Peter called him "a roaring lion in search of someone to devour."[2] And he was not describing a stuffed animal! This is a genuine warfare and serious business of the first degree. God expects us as members within the body of Christ to exercise our dominion over Satan and his cohorts. This authority is part of our throne rights as children of the living God.

I remember well an incident that occurred relatively early in my Christian life. Marilyn and I were invited to spend the night at the home of a friend who lived in a small town about halfway between Chicago and Minneapolis. We were headed home to the Twin Cities for the Christmas holidays, and our friend had asked us to stay overnight with his family with the thought of our sharing the message of Jesus Christ with them.

As we were driving toward the northwest from the Chicago area, a light snow began to fall. By the time we drove into the town where our friend lived a six-inch accumulation of snow had built up, making the decorative lights bridging Main Street warmly accented in their beauty. It was a "Currier and Ives" evening as the pure white snow now blanketed the ground. Following carefully detailed directions, we found a white, wood frame house bordered by a picket fence which beautifully punctuated the already lovely scene. We walked up to the front door and knocked. The door opened, and after an appropriate greeting we entered the living room.

I could not put my finger on what I sensed, but there was some sort of spiritual static in the atmosphere. I had never experienced quite the same feeling. During dinner the subject of Jesus Christ came up in the conversation, and I found myself totally unable to communicate. Later that evening we attended a basketball game in an adjacent town and no one had any fun. The evening was a total bomb.

Later, as we returned home and retired to our room, I became short with Marilyn for no apparent reason. I felt estranged from the presence of God and under some type of spiritual pollution. I could not pray. I tried to analyze what had gone wrong. There seemed to be no reason or explanation for the way I felt.

After a restless and uneasy night we awoke to begin the new day. At the breakfast table I again made an effort to express the love of Christ to this family . . . and nothing. They were tight, I was tight, and the whole situation seemed awkward and tense. I remember when we said good-by I forced myself to say I had enjoyed the stay, but I really did not mean it at all.

Nothing had been accomplished.

As we drove north that morning on the highway bordering the Mississippi River, I thought over the events of the preceding evening. I had no standards of comparison for determining what had happened.

The road was narrow and winding, as it followed the bluffs overlooking the river. Driving itself was tedious because of the many abrupt curves in the road. Finally, the winding highway straightened and we headed inland. We had not progressed more than a few hundred feet from the bluff area when suddenly the rear wheel came off our car! The vehicle swerved toward the right-hand shoulder of the road and ground to a halt. Had that happened thirty seconds earlier, we could have plummeted over the steep cliffs which bordered the river.

I stepped out of the car and breathed a deep sigh of relief. Then I managed to force out a prayer to God to protect me. I *knew* there was something wrong, but there was no way to define it. I asked Him to use the situation we were in for His glory and to get me out from under whatever this gloom cloud was.

There was a small "ma and pa" gas station just a block or so up the road. I told Marilyn to wait in the car. As I walked toward the station, I asked the Lord to allow me to say something to the attendant that would help him to know Christ. The prayer was answered, for as he helped me put the wheel back on the axle, he seemed most receptive to the spoken Word of God.

I felt back on top of it again. The gloom cloud appeared to have lifted.

Two years later a close friend and I were talking in my home in Evanston. He had recently returned from the Orient. As we visited, he began to describe an experience he had the previous year during a stay in Japan. His experience was far more severe in its intensity than mine, but I identified with him as he told of a "gloom cloud" descending upon him during the early days of his visit to that oriental country. He caught me completely off guard, though, when he summed up his remarks by saying, "Pete, I was under a satanic attack."

My mind raced back to our experience on the way to Minneapolis two winters earlier, and I knew there was more to that dilemma than mere happenstance. What before had seemed confusing now came into clear focus. I hated to admit it, but I, too, had experienced the attack of the adversary. And it was no mean thing.

For some, a serious discussion of satanic intervention in human affairs may seem childish and anti-intellectual. To some, what I have said may seem unreal. But don't write it off as child's play. If you have experienced the presence of demonic forces, you know whereof I speak.

A battle is being waged at this very moment, in the realm of the heavenlies, which is real and alive to those who are engaged in the things of the spirit of God. And I am dead serious when I make that statement!

It was Jesus who in describing Satan said, " . . . he was a murderer from the beginning and he could not stay in the truth because there is no truth in him. When he tells a lie he talks naturally; for he is a liar and its father."[3]

Satan lies to us about God. His first recorded words of deceit to mankind were, "Has God *really* said that?"[4] He was the first to employ the "credibility gap" by attempting to take the things God had said and twist them just enough to make them seem false to us.

For example, Satan sends out a charlatan on a faith healing binge with weird music, demonic chants, and a bargain-basement emotional appeal for money and allegiance. This deception is just strong enough that when God comes along with a genuine healing miracle, we voice our doubt and disapproval by saying, "It's all of the devil."

Or, Satan impells us to dismiss the truth of the written Word of God. I cannot count the number of people in their late teens or early twenties with whom I have conversed who are engaged to marry unbelievers. And they already know the passage which commands believers to avoid being unequally yoked with unbelievers.[5]

"This case is different," comes the rationalization. "My boyfriend is right on the verge of trusting Christ. Besides, I prayed about it and have peace." That would be like Noah saying, "I prayed about it and decided not to build the ark after all."

Satan lies to us about the character of God. "If God really loves you," comes the accusation, "then why is He allowing you to go through a period of trial?" Certainly trial is no fun. The Scriptures say it isn't. But James says it produces patience.[6] And Paul says it works out for the good.[7] Instead of looking at the total picture of what God is doing, Satan tries to isolate God's workings to make the whole look bad. The deceiver constantly attempts to involve God in an injustice by getting us to look at the circumstances rather than trusting in Jesus Christ.

Satan began his illustrious career as a created archangel of God. He was the most beautiful creature of God's domain. But he rebelled against God and sought to be like Him. When he fell, a number of the angelic hosts went with him.[8] Jesus said, "And I saw Satan fall from heaven like lightning."[9] This narrative of our Lord was no doubt a reflection upon what the prophet Isaiah had written hundreds of years earlier:

12. How you are fallen from heaven, shining gleam, son of the morning! Chopped down to the ground, conqueror of nations!

13. You reflected in your heart, "I will scale the heavens; I will elevate my throne above the stars of God. I will sit on the mount of assembly, far away in the north.

14. I will rise above the heights of the clouds; I will rival the Most High!"

15. But you will be brought down to Sheol, down to the farthest recesses of the pit.

16. At the sight of you, men will gaze at you and reflect upon you, "Is this the man who caused the earth to tremble, who made kingdoms quake,

17. who turned the world into a desert and overthrew its cities, who would not permit their prisoners to go to their homes?"

18. All the kings of the nations lie in glory, each in his own tomb;

19. but you are cast forth away from your tomb, like a loathed growth, clothed like the slain, pierced by the sword, who go down to the stones in the pit, as a carcass trodden under foot.

20. You will not join your fathers in burial, because you have ruined your country, you have slaughtered your people. May the descendants of evildoers not be mentioned forever!

21. Prepare for his sons a slaughtering place because of their father's guilt, lest they rise up, obtain possession of the earth, and fill the face of the world with cities.

(Isaiah 14:12-21)

Satan has been active throughout history. Jude reports that he disputed with the angel Gabriel over the body of Moses. Even Gabriel did not attempt to take him on alone, but said, "The Lord rebuke you."[10]

Jesus Himself was challenged by the devil during His forty-day fast in the wilderness. The early apostles rebuked Satan repeatedly during their adventures in being used of God to spread the Good News of Jesus Christ. In the Dark Ages Satanic power was vividly present and even worshiped.

Witches and mystic seers have been popular at many varied periods throughout modern history.

And today is no exception. There is a rapidly increasing attempt by Satan and his forces to make what I feel is a last-ditch effort at this particular period in history.

The popular national news magazine *Newsweek* reported recently, "Interest in the occult . . . has suddenly emerged as a mass phenomenon in the United States. Increasing thousands of Americans are now active practitioners of witchcraft, spiritualism, magic and even devil worship. Millions more are addicted to astrology, numerology, fortunetelling and tarot cards."[11]

It is interesting to me that even a secular magazine views these activities as those of Satan's domain, rather than just as hobbies to occupy the leisure mind. The article goes on to say, "What is more significant about the new spiritualism than its rather drab tone is its increased respectability. It may not be too puzzling that millions of otherwise rational, skeptical people now follow the occult avidly from the sidelines."[12]

During the same month *McCall's* featured the explosion in occult activities as its cover story. The lead article contends that " . . . an estimated 40 million Americans, aided by 10,000 professional astrologers, helped turn the zodiac into a $200-million-a-year business." The report further stated that astrology columns are carried in 1,200 of the nation's 1,750 daily newspapers, and that 350 department stores across the country service 30,000 customers each month with "personalized" horoscopes.[13]

Jesus made an interesting assessment of Satan's mission in the tenth chapter of John. In that passage He uses the word "thief" as the figure of speech to describe Satan. In verse ten He says, "The thief comes to steal, to kill, and to destroy." Let's consider for a moment this threefold job description of the enemy.

Satan comes to steal. In the parable of the sower Jesus said, "When anyone hears the message of the kingdom and does not understand it, the evil one comes and snatches away what is sown in his heart."[14] The devil seeks to steal from the work that God has done.

Recently, a young woman who had been deeply involved in hard-core drugs and prostitution was drawn by the Holy Spirit to become a believer in Jesus Christ. Without the presence of a human instrument and without apparent influence from the Scriptures she simply cried out to God and asked Him to take her as His own. The next day the Spirit of God led a person to her who in turn referred her to a close friend of mine for help.

My friend told me how he and his wife had the joy of explaining to her the Cross of Christ, giving her the assurance that the Holy Spirit had come to reside within her. Her experience with satanic influence and demons was so intense that my friends laid hands on her and cast the hindering spirits from her. I was privileged to meet this new, precious sister in Christ the following day.

"When they prayed for me," she related, "it was like a whole load was lifted from me. Satan was like a monkey on my back who fed on drugs. The more I fed him, the hungrier and heavier he became. But Jesus has removed all that."

She told how she had wanted to escape and "go straight" since the age of thirteen when she first began to trip out, but something had a grip on her. "I knew all the drug trips and perversion were a drag, but I could not escape on my own power. I wanted out, but there was no way."

Then she said something that interested me a great deal. "Last night after I was freed from my demonic possession, I went to bed but could not go to sleep. It was as though Satan was standing outside me, begging me to return to his kingdom. I just asked Jesus to keep me covered. I did not want to open my eyes for fear of what I would see. You have no idea of the battle."

Satan did his level best to steal her back from the Kingdom of God, but he failed because Jesus was her Lord.

Most of us do not experience the level of influence by evil spirits that this young lady did. But the lesson here is valid, nonetheless. Satan does everything possible to steal us and our joy in Christ away from the domain of the Godhead. He is a fake! He is without power and authority. He can only lie to us about his power, and does that well. But to listen is to disbelieve the truth which is in Jesus Christ.

Satan comes to kill. This is so obvious in the life-style—or should I say death-style—of the world. Suicide is the number two killer on high school and college campuses, second only to automobile accidents. Part of the devil's stratagem is to try to convince us that because of fear or despair there is no reason to go on living.

Not long ago I was at home having dinner when the telephone rang. On the other end of the line was a friend, a college student, who had been a Christian about a year. He called to report sadly that the man who had led him to Christ —a thirty-five-year-old bachelor—had taken his own life. Satan talked him into doing it. Notice, I did not say Satan killed him—he had no power or authority to do so. But through the big lie, pointing him to the seemingly useless circumstances of life rather than to Christ, the devil convinced him it was futile to continue living.

I was speaking on the campus of one of the most well-known Christian schools in America, an institution where the Bible is consistently taught and upheld and where the students are not admitted to the rolls unless they profess to know Jesus Christ. My subject that evening was our authority, as believers, over Satan.

After my talk, a girl who was known on the campus for her zeal for Christ came up and said, "You won't believe this, but I have been under satanic attack. For several weeks I have seriously contemplated suicide, and tonight I saw for the first time that I have been faked out by Satan. Thank God I am free."

Do you ever entertain thoughts of suicide? Do not listen to Satan's whispers of death. Stand, instead, with the One who conquered death.

Satan comes to destroy. Destruction is his method of altering the affairs of men and nations. War, anarchy, and confusion are the by-products of his harassment of men. God is not the author of confusion. It is Satan who is breeding the mass disarray of today's world system.[15]

You may object at this point and say, "Does that mean that God is against change? There is so much wrong in the world today. Unless there is some type of upheaval, how on earth will things turn around?"

First, the big turn-around is coming when the kingdom of God is revealed. Then, and only then, will we have the type of environment for which all of us long. Don't forget that God started man out in the world's perfect surroundings—paradise. And it was in the garden that man committed his first sin. The problem was in the willing disobedience, not in the environment. Man has tried by his own efforts to improve this earthly scene ever since, and all of us will agree (if we separate morality from technology) that it's become worse and worse.

Second, think back for a moment to God's method for change. He said to the slaves, "Be better slaves."[16] He told the prostitutes to sin no more, but He never tried to wipe out prostitution on a wide scale. His mode of change was diametrically opposed to that of the world. And history bears out that when men allow God to work within them in the environment in which they live, the creative process of God's holy love works wonders in their surroundings. Thus, Paul could write, "Love never fails."[17]

It is important to realize that this present world *is* Satan's domain. He is called the prince of the earth.[18] When he told Jesus that he would give Him the kingdoms of the world if only He would worship him, Satan wasn't kidding.[19] They were—and are—his to give! *Jesus did not challenge his statement.* He knew the "Lame Duck" to whom the world belonged.

We sing "This is my Father's world," and that is true historically and creatively. Satan has swiped the creation from the Creator because we, the creatures, allowed him to do so. When God named us the "called out ones," He meant we were called out of the world, out of the domain of the evil one, into the kingdom of His Son. Therefore, it is the *world* which Satan uses to get at believers: the circumstances, the unbelievers, the events. But in Christ we have authority over Satan and need not put up with his devices.

Before I begin discussing the kind of faith that wins victory over Satan, let me make one more point. As I have used the word Satan in this chapter, I mean not just him individually, but all his "henchmen" and all that he stands for. It would be an ambitious thing for me to assume that it is Satan himself who takes time out from his busy schedule to attempt to work *me* over. As with any effective militia man, he has an army—legions of demons that war with the saints and win with the world. When I talk about a satanic attack, I do not mean to imply that the old man himself gets after you. He is the originator of your troubles, but most likely his personal representatives are the ones who try to overcome you. But just as there are many who are his emissaries, so there are many of us who are the ambassadors of Christ. Jesus has commissioned us to war and win against his forces, and win we shall.

God says we are "mighty through God to the pulling down of strong holds."[20]

A friend once asked me, "Pete, when was the last time you saw a stronghold fall?" At that time I had no answer. But since then the Lord has given ample opportunities to send in the offensive platoon and gain some needed ground.

What is a stronghold? It is any unit of society that belongs to Satan and his influence. It could be a college campus, a social club, or even a group of people who started out as a visible expression of the church, but who no longer trust in Jesus Christ and thus have gone dead. According to the Scriptures we have the power and might together in Christ to see these forces silenced and buried.

Not long ago I was invited to address a huge anti-war rally. It was a stronghold. (Now don't get me wrong—I'm not *for* war! I hate it. It's just that Satan's strategy is to get people to fight each other in an attempt to stop it. And that's exactly what is happening in much of the anti-war effort today.) The crowd bristled with hatred and suspicion. A group of us had prayed the night before and claimed in Jesus' name that Satan would be rebuked and would possess no authority over the throng which had gathered. We claimed the victory before the battle ever began.

Speaking to that group was the toughest thing I had ever done. For the first time in my life, I presented Jesus Christ to a group that was composed of many who openly and vehemently opposed Him. You could sense the tension in the crowd. But the Lord kept the lid on, and for fifteen minutes I told them how the Lord Jesus Christ was the answer to the human dilemma and to their own personal emptiness.

71

God did something in many lives. Some of the instigators of the rally were so mad they couldn't see straight. They were angry at God! Satan had been whipped in their midst, and it was as though they knew it but would never put it into those words. The stronghold was visibly shaken.

I don't know about you, but I don't enjoy getting pushed around. As believers in Jesus Christ, when it comes to the battle in the heavenlies, there is no excuse at all for our getting wiped out. Jesus is Lord. Through Him we lead the procession of triumph.

What are the strongholds you face? The office where you work? Are you afraid to face a group of friends with whom God has led you to share Christ? For some, the stronghold is themselves—a fear of breaking away from self to respond to and obey Jesus Christ. To those of us who are sick and tired of getting sand kicked in our faces, God's Word is "Stand your ground."[21]

Midway through His ministry Jesus was accused by the Pharisees of perhaps the most horrible deed they could have conjured up. They told Him He was casting out demons by the power of Satan.[22] He retorted by saying, "A house divided against itself shall not stand." There is no way for Satan to take a stand against himself. "But," he continued, "if I expel demons through the Spirit of God, then the kingdom of God has overtaken you."

Let me stop here and make a point. Notice, Jesus cast out devils by the Holy Spirit. I am sure many of us have witnessed people who are on a "cast-out-the-demons" kick. It appears fleshly because it is. There are situations (some of which I have already described) in which we need to use our authority in Christ to resist Satan and cast aside demons. But this must be done as the Spirit leads and not to satisfy an ego trip of the flesh. Often there is the temptation to try to repeat by human effort something that God has done earlier through the Holy Spirit. Beware of such counterfeit. As we walk in the Spirit, God will make it clear what He has for us to do.

In Matthew 12:29 Jesus made a statement that changed my confidence and boldness in Him. "How indeed can a person enter into a strong man's house and rob his belongings unless he first binds the strong man? After that he may rob his house." The strong man's house is the same thing we previously called a stronghold. The strong man is Satan. The belongings Jesus speaks of are the furnishings of that house—the goods he has stolen from God and from you and me as members of Christ. His belongings are the people he has taken captive—those for whom Christ died—our beloved friends and relatives whom we so eagerly desire to see come to Christ, but who still stand back and watch with dismay and doubt.

Isn't it about time we move in and start claiming what belongs to us, recapturing the ground we have forfeited? That's what God meant when He said for us to take dominion over the world. God's plan is for us as the body of Christ to move in and strip the devil of his goods!

My blood runs hot when I think of how we as the chosen ones of God have been shoved back for so long by Satan. Doesn't it gripe you to see yourself and/or your friends in Christ living weak, pallid, defeated lives day after day? Where is the power? Where is the authority? Do you care enough to stand up and take the offensive in Jesus Christ?

In Ephesians Paul describes our godly armor.

10. In conclusion, be strong in the Lord and in the strength of His might.

11. Put on the complete armor that God supplies, so you will be able to stand against the devil's intrigues.

12. For our wrestling is not against flesh-and-blood opponents, but against the rulers, the authorities, the cosmic powers of this present darkness, against the spiritual forces of evil in the heavenly spheres.

13. Take up, therefore, the whole armor of God so that you may be able to stand when you have done all the fighting.

14. So stand your ground, with the belt of truth tightened around your waist, wearing the breastplate of righteousness on your body,

15. with the readiness of the good news of peace bound on your feet;

16. above all taking up the shield of faith, with which you will be able to extinguish all the flaming arrows of the evil one.

17. And take the helmet of salvation and the sword of the Spirit, which is the word of God,

18. praying in the Spirit on every occasion with ceaseless prayer and entreaty, constantly alert to pray with all perseverance and entreaty for all the saints.
(Ephesians 6:10-18)

Two things stand out as I read this passage. First, we have armor for every part of our body except the posterior. God has not called the believers to retreat or turn back. Yet that's just what we have been doing! No wonder we are catching the fiery darts of the wicked one. There's nothing back there to protect us! God never intended us or equipped us to be cowards and run.

Secondly, in that whole long list there are only two offensive weapons: the sword of the Spirit, or the *proclaimed Word* of God, and *prayer*. I say "proclaimed word" because that is just what the word picture in the original text implies. You don't win against Satan by passing out Bibles to him and his cohorts. He already believes the written Word. He is defeated as he sees us *speaking* it and *believing* it against him! The written Word is used of God to win people; the spoken Word is used of God to win battles.

Looking ahead to the time of great tribulation, John writes, "And they have conquered him (Satan) by means of the blood of the Lamb and by the word of their testimony."[23] They told of Jesus and claimed Him in their lives. And if the blood of Christ and the witness of the believers overcomes Satan in the great tribulation, *how much more* will he be overcome *now* by those who dare to believe!

Paul wrote that when Jesus disarmed the "rulers and authorities He publicly exposed them to disgrace as He triumphed over them by means of the cross."[24] That is where the "blood of the Lamb" fits in; Satan cannot stand the Cross or the blood of Christ. It was there that Christ dealt him the crushing blow. Thus, as we claim our authority in the Cross and through the blood of Christ, we are reminding Satan that he has no power over us.

Listen—you don't have to put up with him any longer. Jesus cancelled him out. For the child of God, he is a prince without power. Sure, he may make some noise and level some accusations, but don't be content to be a "silent majority Christian." Stand your ground and tell him to scram. "Resist the devil and he *will* flee from you!"[25]

The other weapon of offense is prayer. Frankly, my prayer life is at its best when I know there is something urgent to pray about. That may sound redundant, so let me explain. Normally things go so well that I am not motivated to pray. And that's my fault. That means I've forgotten my privilege of overcoming and am sitting back looking serenely at my not-too-bad environment. But God says we are at war. And "praying at" this battle makes prayer much easier.

If Satan is the prince of the earth, then he is also commander-in-chief of his armed forces. He is top brass—except for one thing. Jesus removed his brass! Thus, he's only top. Which is another way of saying, he's still in the *position* of commander, but he has no *authority* backing up his commands. The true authority in this world has been given by God to the body of Christ!

In an earthly military battle, the best way to win is to destroy the headquarters. Then the lower echelons and forces have no place from which to get their orders, and they scatter in confusion. In a heavenly engagement, it is exactly the same. In Christ, satanic headquarters were knocked out. When we pray to resist Satan, we verbalize our claim of might.

Though I do not fully understand, I have learned one thing about the battle. I pray first and then take my stand against the wiles of the devil. When I go into a situation which I know is a demonic stronghold, I often pray like this:

> Lord Jesus, thank You right this moment that I am covered by Your blood and hidden in the shadow of the Cross. Thank You, Lord, that because I am in You, Satan has no control over me. Now in Your name, Jesus, I resist him in the situation that lies ahead. Rebuke him, Lord. Bind him. Tie him in knots! Thank You in advance that we of your household will triumph over his household. Satan, in Jesus' name, I *command* you to flee.
>
> Lord, I *expect* victory because of what You have promised. Now, Father, by Your Spirit move us ahead

and be powerful within us as we in Your strength possess the land.

What a difference! When Satan is bound, there is no way the cohorts who follow him can know what to do. As he is tied and gagged, we of the mighty kingdom can rush forth and rob him of the goods which beforehand belonged to us. Think of the frame of mind God can create within you as you believe Him for authority over Satan!

*   *   *

What has been said above is strong. Some will have already experienced this truth and will identify readily with what has been said. Perhaps others will see for the first time their position in Christ over Satan and will begin to claim by faith their authority.

Still others may fail to understand and will question the reality of the warfare in heavenly places. If you are among the latter, may I make this suggestion. Don't build your theology on your experience and reject what God says is true. I myself have only experienced a portion of the impact of a satanic attack. Frankly, I do not care to experience more, but I believe God is revealing these truths to prepare me in case He chooses to call upon me for extensive active duty. Let His Word sift through your thinking so that when the occasion comes for you to stand firm against the stratagems of Satan, you will be prepared.

What an honor to emerge with confidence in the victory that is in Christ Jesus our Lord!

Temptation or Desire?

I will put my law in their inward parts, and upon their hearts will I write it.

     — Jeremiah, as he prophesied by the Spirit of God

7

Temptation or Desire?

The problem you encounter with some people when talking about the grace of God is that they somehow feel that the message of freedom in Christ is going to produce license. The major hang-up of those who respond negatively to an emphasis on God's mercy is the fear, they say, that telling people God loves them unconditionally and forgives all their sins will open the floodgates to unrighteousness.

This hesitancy to trust in the grace of God is certainly nothing new. It is interesting to note how often Paul in his epistles says something like, "Shall we remain in sin to let grace become more plentiful? Not at all!"[1] Evidently people in the first century accused Paul of preaching license because frequently after a discourse on grace he would ask that question and proceed to answer it — as if anticipating what people would say.

But what about this issue of people who hear of the grace of God and still keep on sinning? Or even start to sin more? It's really the same issue as that of the person who is given the privilege of believing in Christ and rejects Him. *The problem is not with the message, but with the one who refuses to combine it with faith and accept it.* Let us never fall into the trap of altering the declaration of the Word of God in favor of making it palatable to the ones who don't care to believe it.

In my work in university development I have discovered (or rediscovered) a most interesting phenomenon: when we ask people to invest financially in the ongoing progress of the university and they turn us down, they like to rationalize their negative response. We get letters that say "I saw some hippies on the campus," or "I won't support a school that would elect a black homecoming queen," or "I don't like so and so in the English Department." But when we check the records on these people, we find they have never given a cent anyway. They just wait for an issue to arise and use it as an excuse.

In the same way, people who refuse to accept the Gospel of Christ will begin looking for an excuse to sin. And what better excuse can a person find than to blame the "freedom" found in the message of Christ? And some do! That is why Paul went on to say, "Law is not laid down for an honest person but for the lawless."[2] For you see, the one who rejects the grace of God is forever bound under the law.

Or, some believers say, "If I really believed God loved me regardless of what I'd do, and that in Christ my sins are forgiven forever, I would be afraid of what I would do. I can't trust myself."

Such a conversation happened to me recently. A friend and I were talking about the power of God's love in changing our desires, and the topic of sex arose. "If I as a Christian *really* lived according to my desires," he said, "I'd go out and find some honey and go to bed with her."

Since we were riding alone in a car, I suggested we stop and that he go find someone.

"You know I'd never do it," he responded.

And he wouldn't have either because *he didn't want to.*

He was *tempted* to, but he did not *desire* to.

A beautiful lesson from the Lord: there is a vast difference between our temptations and our desires, if we are truly one with Christ. Satan will lie to us and say that our temptations are reality and that we should obey them. If we believe him and yield to these temptations, soon he will have us thinking they *are* reality and that Jesus cannot change us.

Reality is our new life in Jesus Christ. "Have your delight in the Lord and He will give you the desires of your heart."[3] I see two things in this passage. First, God will give us the desires He wants us to possess — a new set of want-to's. Often when a person initially puts his trust in Christ, he previously has been rather far out to sea morally. God promises to reprogram him to fit his new life. Secondly, God will fulfill these desires. He'll give us what our new life truly wants.

The more we learn to trust in the reality of Jesus Christ, the more we will desire Him and the things His life produces, and the less sway temptation will hold over us. We will see Christ more and more as real peace and true joy, and we will view temptation more and more as the drag that it surely is.

Temptation is manifest from three basic areas: the world, the flesh, and the devil.[4] All three say, in effect, "I want you to establish your identity with me." The world calls us to become part of its flow — to advance in it, to receive its honors and laurels. It is a sub-kingdom that has excluded God.

The flesh pleads for satisfaction — quick and exhilarating living for the moment at the expense of all else.

Satan, as a fake deity, tempts us by promises which cannot come true.

These three enemies work together to form a full-orbed program of temptation which to the child of God is unreal, unenjoyable, unprofitable and, in a word, death. Temptation plagued us before we believed, and it will hang around after, but its power over us as we resist in Christ Jesus becomes less and less.

Desire, on the other hand, comes from God. It is definitely present after we believe, and perhaps it is on hand in some form or other before we believe, too. I desired the Lord and His life before coming to know Him, but my life was still in the world of deceptions. Temptation is accompanied by confusion; the will of the Lord and the desires of our hearts are characterized by steady inner peace. I find in my experience that increasingly I am rejecting temptation and accepting the reality of Christ. The more I dwell in His life, the less I enjoy world-life.

One day I telephoned home from work to visit with Marilyn. She began telling me how everything was going wrong that day. Then she said, "I should be discouraged, but I told the Lord that I am rejecting discouragement in His name. And you know, it works! I *should* be down, but I'm not." She went on to praise Him.

That incident has come back to me over and over again. You reject death and receive life! She was *tempted* to be down, but her *desire* was to be up.

Discouragement is preoccupation with self. Praise, on the other hand, is preoccupation with the Lord Jesus. Temptation is the call to live according to times past, depending on the world, the flesh, or even on the will of Satan. When we are in Christ, our desires come from the Lord Himself and are in harmony with His will.

You say, "But what about those areas which I cannot distinguish? What if I'm not sure whether it's from the Lord or not?" There's a simple answer to that. You *wait* on the Lord. Let me say it again because I love the word and the way it sounds — *wait!*

Let's be thoroughly non-theological. Let's call this twilight zone in between desires and temptations *impulses*. I *act* on my desires from the Lord, *refuse* my temptations, and *wait* on my impulses. Often my impulses are really desires that come ahead of the Lord's timing. Other times they are from the flesh and soon disappear.

Let me use another example. Both Marilyn and I, as I said in an earlier chapter, would love to have an old home in the country. But neither of us has peace about making a move. So we're having a great time just waiting. A few years ago, before understanding that the Lord gives us the desires of our hearts, waiting would have been synonymous with frustration. But knowing that He is running the show, it has become a joy (at least in this instance!) to wait.

One afternoon we drove out to a small town east of Memphis to look at a pre-Civil War house on fourteen acres of wooded land. I could have afforded to make the move, but there was no peace. So while the impulse to move to the country remains, the light flashes "wait."

Maybe we will get there someday; maybe we will never get there. But whether we do or not, we have peace. And that's *such* a great feeling.

I am sure all of us can look back to a time — perhaps recently — when we disobeyed God and went ahead on something that was not of Him. What happens then? God says He'll work it out for good. He may use it to teach you to obey Him in the future. Certainly He'll use it to change your want-to's.

Recently I was with a person who had disobeyed not long ago. He said, "If another Christian had stood up and told me not to, I would still be doing it. But now that the Lord has said no, that's it."

There is a beautiful freedom in obedience to God. He alone is reality. Because of the fact that Christ is our life, we have the capability of "gettin' it all together" and *experiencing* a walk within His leading and within His will. I guess that's why Paul wrote, "If God is for us, then who is against us?"[5]

When the Bottom Falls Out

*For I consider that the sufferings of this present time
are not worthy to be compared
with the glory that is to be revealed in us.*

— Paul of Tarsus

8

When the Bottom Falls Out

We have considered the privilege we possess as the people of God of being a part of God's Master Plan. When we were in the world, our lives in many ways were affected by the finiteness and pressure of the world system. Though the Spirit of God was no doubt at work within us to draw us to Christ, nonetheless we were generally without any real direction or destiny as far as God was concerned.

But now that situation has changed. As members of the body of Christ we have been brought into a plan or moving or life-flow of the Lord which, as we have seen, is taking us from our present place to the great City of our God. There are many ramifications resulting in our lives from this truth. Let us consider one about which all of us will most likely need to know a great deal more as the days pass. I am speaking of the way in which we can count upon the Lord when tribulation and heartbreak occur. In Christ we are strong to stand when the bottom falls out.

As a new believer, I was merely comforted to know of Romans 8:28. As a more mature believer, I am liberated beyond description by its message: "But we know that for those who love Him, for those called in agreement with His purpose, God makes all things work together for good."[1]

For me, this has been the most basic lesson I ever learned. Think of making it through what appear to be setbacks or disappointments. I can remember blowing an exam which I had studied for carefully and then realizing that somehow, someway the Lord was still working everything together for good.

Such simple lessons are embodied in this verse. God says *all* things work together for good. Major or minor, happy or sad, permanent or temporary — His promise is that we are not left to chance or happenstance. Everything is working together toward His purpose.

The Lord does not say all things or events *are* good, but He does insure that all things work together *for* good. In the Old Testament we have His promise that He shall use even the wrath of men to praise Him.[2] I have seen repeatedly where an individual has set out deliberately to destroy or discredit the work of the Lord and wham — the whole scene changes. I believe that often God allows the bad mouths to sound off so that people will see the difference and choose Christ.

The real meaning of "All things working together for good" hit me between the eyes just the other night. A friend was talking with a large group of college students, attempting to answer their questions. Many in the group were not believers. One of the adamant nonbelievers started to bait the speaker with questions which were designed as a trap. My friend caught what was happening, lost his temper momentarily and said some things to the students that he later regretted. One girl became so upset, she left the roon in a huff.

As we were driving home, he apologized for his display of anger. I quoted Romans 8:28 to him almost out of the force of habit, failing to see the impact of what I was repeating.

The following day, the girl who had stormed out of the room placed her faith in Christ. This is what had happened:

When she left in disgust the night before, a Christian girl had followed her out to explain and make restitution. The two girls agreed to meet for coffee the next day, and it was during this time that the upset coed gave her life to Jesus Christ. God worked even an unwarranted display of anger for good, for had that situation not occurred, humanly speaking that girl may never have come to know Christ.

In light of this great verse another spiritual truth takes on strong meaning. Paul wrote in First Thessalonians 5:18 (KJV), "In every thing give thanks: for this is the will of God in Christ Jesus concerning you." If we really are convinced that God is working all things that happen to His children together for good, then the inevitable response will be to offer thanks whether we understand the circumstances or not.

It is easier for me to agree inwardly when something adverse happens than it is for me to come right out and say "Thank You" to Him. I have discovered, though, that if you give thanks for good things that happen, it is much easier to give thanks when the bottom falls out.

The first time I remember saying "Thank You" for an adversity came after I had been a Christian about two years. One night Marilyn and I were taking a friend to our house for dessert. We were almost home.

I was approaching a blind corner and slowed down to make sure another car was not coming through the intersection from either direction. It looked clear so I accelerated, but a man shot through the "yield right of way" sign to our right and we hit him broadside. I looked at his car on my front bumper and was scared to death. We had hit with solid impact, and I counted five people in the other car.

As I opened my door to get out to see if I could help the others, I said, "Thank You, Lord," audibly. But it was not my flesh that said it. It was my spirit responding to the Spirit of God. I'll never forget that incident because it was a milestone in my spiritual life. Hot-tempered me had said "thanks" to the Father, and I knew it was because He had changed me.

The eight of us were checked over at the hospital, and five of us were released. The other three were treated for typical injuries resulting from this type of accident and were discharged a few days later. Everyone lost on the deal in terms of time, bother, and money. Both cars were total wrecks. I still do not know why it happened, but I did discover the truth of saying "Thank You."

The Scriptures also talk about offering up a sacrifice of praise.[3] We read, "Enter into His gates with thanksgiving and into His courts with praise."[4] A friend recently said, "Praise is the language of heaven. Let us exercise it often so we will not be tongue-tied when we arrive." I love that!

Slowly the Lord is overcoming a barrier in my life. Traditionally, I have been afraid to praise Him in front of others. It was a huge breakthrough for me to unashamedly mention the name of Jesus Christ in public. Occasionally I still have trouble, but generally boldness has become more natural.

But sounding forth with praise is something different. I am just beginning to see that God is glorified when praise resounds to Him from His people on the earth. Desiring to glorify Him, I want to be part of this chorus of celebration and praise. It defaces the flesh and human reputation, I am learning, to praise Him without regret or hesitation. But it's coming, and life in Him gets better every day.

I have known little in the way of spiritual or emotional trial. I have never lost a child or had problems in marriage. There have been a few times of financial strain, but nothing which even approached being in want. I have never been without work. I have not known the emptiness of being deserted by friends. But in the little things our confidence and trust grow so that when the big things come Christ will be sufficient.

The Psalms are a tremendous reservoir of encouragement for times of trouble. One of the most meaningful passages I have found is in Psalm 91:

14. Because he has anchored his love in Me, I will deliver him. I will place him securely on high, for he has faith in My name.

15. When he calls upon Me, I will answer him; I will be with him in trouble; I will rescue him and honor him.

16. I will satisfy him with a long life and show him My salvation.   (Psalm 91:14-16)

For a typical man in today's world it seems there are three stages he passes through in his adult life. As he finishes his school years and begins a career, he seeks *security*. He wants to know what his salary will be and the particulars on side benefits. As he matures and advances in his work, his interest turns to *power*. "How big is my responsibility?" he asks. "What are the opportunities to effect a change?" The number of people reporting to him often becomes an issue. In the autumn of his life he seeks the third and final phase: *honor*. He has succeeded in earning security, he has been given a share of power, and now it is recognition he desires. For without some sense of acclaim, the other two now matter little.

These three steps are the plight of the citizen of the world. But I wonder if these are not basic hungers God has placed within us which apply to our relationship with Him and His Kingdom.

In Christ, we really need security. When I was still a young Christian, a skeptic said to me, "You've taken Jesus like a crutch."

It made me angry.

After some years of walking with the Lord, if he would say that to me today, my reply would be, "You're exactly right." Sure, Jesus is more than a crutch. But in the sense that I am weak and need someone strong to make me strong, He is a crutch. His security is beautiful—both in our early days with Him when He promises, "I will not give you up nor desert you,"[5] and in our later years when in times of trial we hear, "Come to Me all you who labor and are heavily burdened, and I will give you rest."[6]

Then there's power. I read, "Be strong in the Lord and in the strength of His might,"[7] and my heart says, "That's the way I want to be." It's not that I want power to step all over people and get my way, but I do want to know by experience that dominion which I was created to possess. As a new Christian, I needed security; today I wish to live in His power and say with Paul, "I have strength for every situation through Him who empowers me."[8]

There will come a day when I need neither security nor power. In the New Jerusalem those two will have slipped on by, for there I shall know honor and glory. And that is just what He has promised! That is what the whole business of rewards is all about — God bestowing His honor upon us.

Look again at the portion of Psalm 91. When the bottom falls out, God will deliver us. When we need security and power, He promises, "I will place him securely on high." On high is the place of power! And then, when we call, He answers. Let me expand on that for a moment.

Sometimes — not always — God allows our plans and dreams to be sidelined for a special gracious reason: He wants to get our attention. Can you relate to what I say when I tell you that at times I get so busy I just blast through life and politely ignore Him? Then — boom! A problem arises and He has my undivided attention. I start praying and asking Him for answers — and the answers come. I look back on the experience and fail to see how it fits into what must be His overall plan. Often I conclude He allowed it just so He could hear from me.

What a merciful Father, to take time out like that just to attract me back into a conversational relationship.

When we need help, God says, "I will be with him in trouble; I will rescue him . . . ." Let's file that away under "Readily Accessible" for future use.

Finally the Psalmist records, "I will . . . honor him. I will satisfy him with a long life and show him my salvation." When you see the end of things, you can go through virtually anything to get there. When I see what God has prepared for those who love Him, everything along the way seems hardly worthwhile taking into account.

Regardless of the circumstances now, God promises us honor, satisfaction, and salvation! Can you think of any way to improve that? What else really counts? No wonder Paul had the courage to say, "For I am convinced that neither death nor life, neither angels nor authorities, neither present nor future affairs, neither powers of the heights nor of the depths, nor anything else created will be able to separate us from the love of God that is in Christ Jesus our Lord."9 What else really matters?

Besides honor, He promises satisfaction for the length of our lives. Wow! As a nonbeliever I used to sweat death and wonder what on earth I could do with my life to make it significant. Now earth-life is not the issue. A friend in Memphis said to me recently, "The more I grow in the Lord, the more I see that physical death is not all that big a deal." God says whatever the length of our lives, we will be satisfied with what He gives us, for real life never ends.

When troubles used to come, I would always try to analyze "why." That doesn't get it anymore. I don't *care* why. I am learning, slowly, that what happens to me is God's business. He is working it together for good; He asks me to simply thank Him and see that because of what is ahead *my* head should be there instead of only here!

The Experience of Rest

The Lord your God is settling you here. He is giving you this land.

— Moses

9

The Experience of Rest

How do you transfer the power which is ours in Jesus Christ into the "time line" where we all live? If we have all the authority and dominion from the right hand of God that He says we do, how does this affect the way we spend our time?

It seems to me that the new crop of believers who have come to Christ in recent years do not have nearly the problem with this that some of us do who have been around a bit longer. As I look at those of us who are thirty or above, I see what I define as "poor balance" in the way we live our lives. There is that minority, on one hand, who are so deeply involved in Christian "activity" that everything else suffers. They are gone too much, are too tired, are always "giving out" instead of "taking in," and are constantly setting up new programs "for the Lord." I tend to fall in this category.

Then there is what appears to be a burgeoning majority who scarcely do a lick. They exhibit the "spiritual blahs."

Sure, they could give a brief testimony of faith if they were asked, but their enthusiasm and life-throb is missing.

Finally, there is a small group with balance. By *balance* I do not mean humanly designed usage of time and talent. This group just seems to be able to walk in the Spirit without getting either ahead of the Lord or behind Him. Using Biblical language, they have "entered into His rest." They operate from a position of rest rather than from an orientation of either laziness or frazzled activity.

Two passages in the New Testament deal directly with what we are discussing here. The first is found in the first few verses of Hebrews 4. The other is in I Timothy.

THE REST OF GOD

The context of Hebrews 4 is the forty-year wilderness wandering experience of the children of Israel. There is no reason why the Israelites could not have walked right out of Egypt, through the wilderness, and directly into the Land of Promise. It is at most an eight- to eleven-day journey by foot through the wilderness area, but it took them forty years! God says they failed to enter into their Promised Land the first time because of unbelief. They did not trust the Lord when He said He would give them strength and wisdom to take the land. So they chose forty years of useless, man-made activity instead of claiming God's promise that "the Lord will fight for you while you keep still."[1] God had *promised* them a land where they could relax in Him and see their needs and the needs of others met, but they chose instead to live by works instead of faith. And thus we read in Hebrews:

1. Let us then be on our guard so that, while the promise of entering into His rest still holds, none of you may be found to be delinquent,

2. for we have had the good news preached to us, just as they did. But the message they heard did not benefit them, because it was not united by faith to those who heard it.

3. For we who have believed enter into His rest, as He has said, "As I swore in My anger, they shall not enter into My rest"; although His works had been accomplished from the foundation of the world.

4. For somewhere He says this about the seventh day, "And God rested on the seventh day from all His works," and again in this passage, "They shall not enter into My rest."

(Hebrews 4:1-4)

To show us what He means, God compares the rest He has for us with the rest He Himself experienced after His creation was finished. He worked for six days and entered into rest on the seventh.

In our case, however, God does not even ask us to work the first six days! His point is that the work that needs to be done is finished. He will work through those who belong to Him to *apply* His finished work in areas where it is needed, but the actual work itself has been accomplished.

The Israelites began their journey in Egypt, the place the Scriptures symbolically picture as "the world." There they were in confusion and spiritual estrangement. When they moved out of Egypt, they were headed not for the wilderness, but directly for the Promised Land. The wilderness had never been a live option for them at the outset; that which had been intended to be merely a brief stepping stone to the Land of Promise became a stone of stumbling for them which lasted four decades. They took what God had intended as the *means* and made it their veritable *end*.

Our human activity is the means, not the end, of perceiving and experiencing divine life—the life of Jesus Christ. Thus, the things we *do*—our production, our activity—are not really what God is after in an ultimate sense at all. He wants us—as *He* has—to cease from wilderness activity and to simply rest. A synonym for rest is "believe" or "live by the life of Christ."

Living by Jesus' life is living in the Land of Promise. And in the land, the work that God has done from the foundation of the world is the basis of all that happens there. We become vessels; He becomes our strength.

RESTING IN A HECTIC WORLD

Accepting the principle of rest into our daily experience, the passage in First Timothy clearly offers some beautiful direction:

1. First of all, then, I urge that petitions, prayers, intercessions, and thanksgivings be made for all people,

2. for kings and all who hold high positions, that with all reverence and dignity we may lead a quiet and undisturbed life.

3. This is good and acceptable before God our Savior,

4. who wants all persons to be saved and to come to the knowledge of the truth.

(I Timothy 2:1-4)

Paul begins by asking us to pray for political leaders. This is something I have begun doing just recently. I want to do it more because I am beginning to see a reason for it. The emphasis in this passage is not to pray that they might find new life in Christ, though that is a most valid way to pray. Nor is it the emphasis of the apostle to have us pray for them that national political freedom might prevail.

The kind of prayer described here is what some might even call "selfish" prayer. Paul asks us to pray for kings and leaders so that we, the people, may lead a "tranquil and quiet life in all godliness and dignity" (ASV).

Let's take that into the practical realm for a moment. How many Christians do you know who are leading a

    tranquil and
    quiet life
    in all godliness
    and dignity?

There just aren't many. And perhaps one reason there aren't more is that we have forgotten that God *really* wants us to live that way. We hear so many "urgency of the hour" messages. Have we forgotten that it is the Holy Spirit—not the urgency of the times—who is supposed to motivate and control our lives?

Certainly we live in an urgent period of history. Almost everyone would agree to that. But Paul lived in urgent days, too. Yet he preached, "The love of Christ lays hold of (motivates) us."[2] He did not hold the threat of political suppression over them to urge them on. The religious and political leaders had *already* told the believers to shut up, and they spread the word all the more!

If we let the world situation, as opposed to the Lord Jesus Christ, dictate the way we should live our lives, we are allowing ourselves to be moved by fear.

Regardless of social circumstances, regardless of the hectic life-style of the world, regardless of the need of the hour—as undeniably real as they may be—*our lives are to be lived in the power and fullness of the Holy Spirit and in Him alone.*

TRANQUILLITY

The Greek word was taken from an adverb meaning "quietly," and my mind pictures something almost like Walden's Pond. Peaceful. The world going bananas around it maybe, but peaceful.

Where is that element among our generation of believers? Generally speaking, it is nonexistent. I am not talking about laziness here. That's as much of the flesh as busy-ness for busy-ness' sake. Nor do I mean simply an outlook or attitude of tranquillity which never seeps through to the level of experience. I mean tranquillity in the very center of our lives.

I wonder if it isn't the busy lives of our current crop of middle-aged parents that has caused so much of the estrangement that kids say they feel.

Recently I was conversing with a college senior at one of our large state universities and we hit on the subject of family life. From his background, I had assumed he came from an outstanding home. But his evaluation of his home differed markedly from what I expected him to relate.

"One thing for sure," he said, "I don't care to be like my dad."

"How do you mean?" I asked.

"I don't know the man," he answered. "He's too busy. Monday night he usually entertains clients or participates in other activities of his company. Tuesday night is civic and community affairs. Wednesday night is the church board or choir. Thursday night is bowling. Friday and Saturday nights he and mom hit the social circuit, and he plays golf or works out at the club Saturday during the day. Sunday is church, yard work, and TV. I've never gotten to know him.

"Dad's whole goal," he continued, "is to be president of his company. And he'll make it, too. All he has to do is outlive the man at the top and by Las Vegas odds, he's in. But to do it, he's had to sacrifice his time at home to look good around town and at the office.

"I just don't care to be like that. When I get married, I'm going to work to provide for my wife and kids, but deliver me from the rat race. It's just not worth it."

That was a sermon I needed to hear. I was with him all the way.

This kid is by no means a "drop out." He just put into words something that probably most of us have felt but have seldom verbalized.

QUIET

The word *quiet* here means "hushed" or "internally gentle." The only other place this particular word is used in the New Testament is in First Peter 3:4 where it is employed to describe a mode of behavior opposite from that of being "showy" or "external."

As far as the Lord's people are concerned, this is the same basic truth that God was trying to convey back in First Kings when He talked about the Temple being constructed without the sound of an ax or hammer.

For the Church of Jesus Christ to be built, human noise just isn't necessary. God wants the human stones which comprise His "temple made without hands"[3] to be molded and hewn by the Holy Spirit. If God calls me to holler and shout, may I do so with fervor. But my orientation to the Land of Promise is that of quietness, of being still and knowing He is God.

GODLINESS

This is simply being filled with and obedient to the life of God. It is living out our oneness with Jesus Christ—that state of being which allows the Holy Spirit freedom to lead us.

Godliness is not a complicated thing. It couldn't be or ordinary people could never get it. It is simply letting Jesus be our life.

A student from Chicago said something to me recently which I believe really communicates godliness.

As we visited one day, he said, "I don't want Jesus Christ to be first in my life anymore."

I'm sure I looked at him with a puzzled expression.

"If He's first in my life," he continued, "then that pre-supposes there must be other things second and third and fourth and fifth. If that is true, then these other things will be vying for first place. I just want Him to *be* my life."

DIGNITY

A general translation of this word would communicate something like "sincerity" or "reverence." It embodies the idea of possessing praise in our hearts for the Lord or simply loving Him back for all that He has done for us.

Dignity and reverence (or worship) are not big formal things. They are the spontaneous response of a person or group of persons whose lives belong to Christ. They proceed out of the life of the Spirit.

THE ATMOSPHERE IS DIFFERENT

You see, the "tranquil and quiet life in all godliness and dignity" is the direct opposite of human life. This is the same quality of life we will know when we go to be with God. He tells us what it will be like so we will have the opportunity to practice it before we arrive. This tranquillity is the atmosphere of the new heaven and the new earth; it's different!

The problem is that I am so accustomed to living world-type life that I find it difficult to allow the Lord to attune me to spiritual life. It's that old "urgency" bit again.

But God is really serious when He says that He wills us to live a tranquil and quiet life in all godliness and dignity. So much so that He follows that sentence with this one: "this is good and acceptable before God our Savior." It is almost as though He expects us to balk when He tells us to rest, so He immediately endorses what He has said as being just what He wants.

We "activists" object and say, "This peaceful and tranquil stuff may be fine for some, but I've got a job to do. I'm too involved to live this way. I'm dedicated to be a 'one hundred percenter.' I've got several Bible studies or koinonia groups going each week to reach my neighbors. Then there are all my activities at church, plus my noon luncheons and rap sessions. I'm so caught up, there's no way I can stop."

Look what God says in verse 4: "who wants all persons to be saved and to come to the knowledge of the truth."

And that's the whole point.

Men are not going to be reached if all the Christians are running around like proverbial chickens with their heads cut off, trying to hustle everyone into the Kingdom. What is the difference between the life of the guy who is out six or seven nights a week "making it" socially and in business while his family goes down the drain and the guy who is out every night of the week "winning the world" while *his* marriage begins to crumble and his kids rebel?

Do you know what the world needs (and secretly wants) to see? A body of believers who are living quiet, tranquil, godly, humble lives—whose Lord leads them to stay home where they belong, in love with their spouses and children; who are free to talk with, listen to, and understand their friends and neighbors; who are not all hung up on pushing the Gospel at the expense of living it and enjoying it—believers who are just God's *people*, rather than His big-time leaders and hustlers.

Am I saying this kindly and gently enough to communicate? It is when we are willing to die to our activity and our programs and just become the Lord's people again that the Spirit will be free to really work. Laying my self-appointed "Christian activity" on the altar to be burned was one of the most difficult things I have ever done. Because, you see, I still *cared* about people coming to know Jesus Christ. My desire to have the world hear the Good News had not changed at all, and it still has not today. I was so afraid that if I ceased my "spiritual" works and entered into the rest of the Lord that God could not use me. But it was after getting un-busy and turning my time back over to Him that He began to use me in much greater depth than I had ever known previously.

There's no program left for me to push anymore—no need to put people into a preconceived mold I had made for them. I still present the Gospel in public, but it is out of life rather than duty. I probably talk with several people each day about Christ, but I don't stop and count anymore because it is not an isolated "talking" thing opposed to "helping" or "loving" or something else. Since I have stopped *trying* to produce spiritual action, far more true fruitfulness has resulted. I have never known a richer experience of seeing people respond and grow in Jesus Christ than I have since I sacrificed my activity. What a release to be free!

And attitudes—the joy of being at home without guilt! Or of being able to say *"no"* because I'm "too busy" or "Tonight I'm staying home."

Lord Jesus, I ask You not only to be my life, but also be my schedule. I resign to You my trying to keep un-busy as well as my trying to do enough. Lord, I see more every day that "trying" is wilderness life, and I despise it.

I will to You my calendar, my wrist watch, my desk-pad, my telephone, and all the other creations of men that place our attention on the means instead of the end. Strip me of activity, Father. Give me the boldness—the guts—to say "no" and mean it when another committee asks me to serve and You tell me to decline.

And yet, Lord, give me Your sensitivity and discernment so that when my brother is in need, and I am Your chosen instrument to meet his need, I will unselfishly run to his side.

Lord, deliver me from slavery to the TV and to "keeping pace" with whatever—besides You—tends to motivate my way of life. Thank You for the freedom You offer and for the way You are restoring my soul. I claim all that You are right now, as I recognize the transfer of title of my life from me to You. Thank You, Lord Jesus, for liberating me to trust You and to thrive on Your life within me. Amen.

We Really Are One

*Behold, how good and how pleasant it is
for brethren to dwell together in unity!*

— David

10

We Really Are One

A powerful characteristic of eternal life or divine life is that we are all *one* fellowship, *one* body in Jesus Christ. If we have this life of Christ which is eternal right now, as we say we do, then where in the world is all that oneness?

Let us suppose I am an unbeliever and am reading your New Testament. I come across some underlined passages that read, "That all may be one, as Thou Father art in Me, and I in Thee,"[1] and "By this everyone will recognize that you are My disciples, if you love one another."[2] I ask, "Where *is* all this unity?" What would be your reply?

This oneness business is not an option. It is part of the plan — God's plan. Whatever happened to it?

It is my feeling that we *learn* segregation from one another. Remember back to your early days as a believer? You had no problem accepting others who were born of God like you. But if you are like most people, sectarianism got a hold on you.

As a new Christian, I had no problem accepting others who named the name of Jesus Christ. It was the natural thing to do. Sectarianism had never been an issue.

ONENESS IS NOT GIFTS OR GOALS

But in becoming part of a religious system, I began to adopt the biases upon which that structure was founded. Our particular group was built around the spiritual gift of evangelism, and it is a great gift. But, you see, the only thing Jesus ever established as an expression of Himself to the world was His body of believers called the Church. Instead of being centered around Christ first, we were centered around the evangelization of mankind. But if you had asked us, we would have said we were centered around Christ and Him alone.

Now evangelism, as I said, is a wonderful gift, but it is not the basis of oneness. We all would have agreed to that, but we were still centered around evangelism. And here was the ramification: we could not bring into our structure those whose views of evangelism were not exactly what ours were. It would water us down, we said. And it *would have.* Because when your center is anything besides oneness in the Lord Jesus, it is easy to get watered down.

Also, we automatically rejected those who had the gift of tongues. This we saw as a movement in conflict with our own, and we were absolutely correct. Because if one group is built around one gift and another group around another gift, there is bound to be conflict. But if we can die to our allegiance to gifts and hold only to Jesus Christ, where on earth can the conflict be?

Today I believe in evangelism as deeply as I ever have — in fact, more so. But my life is no longer built around it. God told me to unstructure myself, and I obeyed. Since some who will read this may be curious about tongues — no, I have never spoken in tongues. Possession of a gift, whatever it is, is not the point. If you have spoken in tongues, fine. Though I do not experience the gift, I love you and cherish you as a brother or sister in Jesus Christ.

Please don't try to get me into your gift though, whatever it may be, and I won't attempt to get you into mine. We are being built up into *Christ* — not tongues, evangelism, teachings, prophecy, or whatever. Jesus alone is head of the body.

ONENESS IS NOT ORGANIZATIONAL

It seems I keep running into full-time ministers who are losing their desire to push their denominations. All they want is to be brothers in Christ. Some of them know that ultimately they will have to leave their ministries because the structures they represent will not tolerate the "disloyalty" of not emphasizing favorite cornerstones upon which the denominations were founded. These men want Christ to be the cornerstone so they can be built up together with others who know Jesus whether their doctrines coincide or not. And they may have to leave. I had to leave. The hard part was that I intensely loved and still do love the people I left, but to be free to be one with all believers I had to first step outside of the structure of a few.

Let me hasten to say that just because a person is identified with structured Christianity does not at all imply he has a weak love for Jesus Christ. Huge numbers of people within the gates love Him to death! And I have found that most people associated with organized religion are transparently honest in agreeing that they, of necessity, must avoid intimate oneness with a portion of other believers with whom they cannot doctrinally or philosophically relate. Virtually all who work with extra-church organizations will say that if the Church were really functioning as it ought, their reason for existing organizationally would be eliminated.

I wish to accept people, be they in or out of structured religion. And, generally, I have found that people out of the structure can potentially be one with all who belong to Jesus Christ because they have no boundary other than Jesus Christ — whereas many within the system can fellowship completely only with those who are in the established limits of their system.

I have to say this because I believe God wants me to say it: He is calling people *out* of sectarianism and *out* of systems which men have built who declare that we can join them if we do so on their terms.

You may say, "Well, Gillquist, what you say is a system, too. You're talking about a oneness that denies a structure; therefore your basis of fellowship is in having no structure at all."

Jesus sees the church as His body. Man says you need to put the body of Christ into a container. You must put it into something people can see and define, he maintains. But the only type of body that needs a container is a dead body. A live body is its own container. May I repeat that? A live body is its own container. The beautiful attribute of something alive is that it is free from needing a structure to contain it or to limit it. *It just lives!!!*

If I were to say to a live person lying in a coffin, "For you to live to the fullest, you should get out of the casket to be free to move," he might challenge me by saying the universe is a kind of container too. In a way he'd be right. I'd most likely just excuse myself and walk on and find something else to do, rather than try to convince him of something he didn't really care to know.

Sure, a live person can survive in a container.

When I say these things, people often think I hate folks who are bound to organized religion. How could I do that, when the Lord says I'm one with all brothers everywhere? I want to love people regardless of their identity structurally. It's up to the Lord to lead us, not me. I am merely attempting to verbalize what He has done with *my* life and to relate its significance to the patterns of *our* lives.

If God's overall plan was simply to get people "saved," evangelism *would* be our reason for being. If His main purpose was to get people "socially concerned," then community involvement *would* be our thing. If He primarily wanted people as educated as possible in Bible facts, then *that* is the route we would take. If His favorite doctrine was the favorite doctrine of one of the (how many hundred?) Christian denominations, then by all means, that would be the one to join.

You see, all the above can be parts of the whole, but they are not the whole. We get what the body of Christ *does* confused with what it *is*. "There is *one* body and *one* Spirit, just as also you received your calling, with *one* hope; *one* Lord, *one* faith, *one* baptism; *one* God and Father of all, who governs all and pervades all and is in us all,"[3] (italics mine), Paul said.

The issue is not, "We have a job to do." The battle is the Lord's. Nor is the issue to try for oneness. God says we are already one.

God has begun only one thing: the Body of His Son. All the rest proceeds from that. We cannot add to or subtract from it. The real question is this: am I in a position in this life to be drawn by Him to the point where I can begin to *experience* and *live* that oneness He says already exists? I was not ready, and for me the impediment had to go. My big road-block was structure, and it went. My little roadblocks are within me, and I find myself being stripped of them as the days and weeks go by.

ONENESS IS NOT DOCTRINAL AGREEMENT

The less I grow in Christ, the more concerned I am about what you believe. The more I grow, the less concerned I am. I have ideas on baptism, prophecy, the church, gifts, attitudes which I believe to be true. But common doctrine is not the key to oneness.

After my first book, *Love Is Now*, was published, a number of letters came each week. The ones I dug the most were those which said something like, "Isn't our Lord great?" or "Jesus Christ has become so real to me," or "I love the Father and my brothers and sisters." The ones that hurt were those which said, "I agreed with your position on . . ." or "I did not agree with your views on . . . ."

I don't want people to rally around what I may say either in agreement or disagreement. Let's just rally around Christ. As we relinquish our lives to Him, the Holy Spirit, on the promise of Jesus Himself, "will guide you into all truth."[4]

There is a life far higher than living by what we may think is doctrinally right or wrong. That life is the life of Jesus Christ Himself — He *is* life. We cannot divide over Him if we take our life from Him. In Him we will find righteousness and possess it. His life is one life, so our lives in Him are one life. God ultimately will destroy *all* that seeks to divide us. The writer of Proverbs warned against living with a contentious woman,[5] and certainly Jesus will not continue to put up with a bickering bride!

ONENESS IS NOT A HUMAN LEADER

Jesus' dislike for human headship was the basis for most of His gripe with the Pharisees and the Sadducees. He became, as we say here in the South, right indignant!

42. But Jesus summoned them and said to them, "You know how those supposed to govern the Gentiles lord it over them, and their great men exert authority over them;

43. but this is not your way. Instead, whoever wants to be great among you will be your servant,

44. and whoever wants to be first among you will be everyone's slave.

45. For even the Son of Man did not come to be served but to serve and to give His life a ransom for many."
(Mark 10:42-45)

Comparing the philosophy of world-related leadership, and how it affects unity among people, with spiritual oneness, He said in principle, "Don't do it the way the world does it." He told those who wished to "minister" just to be servants. No titles, offices, or ranks — just servitude. *And He used Himself as the example!*

Now, certainly, as we function together, those with gifts and spiritual callings will become obvious, thus promoting order and authority. But in the reality of our fellowship we are one and equals in Jesus Christ and not under human office or position.

There is a great difference between those to whom *God* has given spiritual authority and those who have received an appointment by the ecclesiastical systems of the establishment. God calls some to be evangelists, pastors, and teachers, and He names elders, prophets, and apostles. This is done through His Spirit. There is authority in these people — not vested by organizations, but placed within them by the Holy Spirit.

Those of God's choosing do not have to hang out shingles which say, "I have spiritual authority." Believers who walk with them in the bonds of the Holy Spirit know that they have it.

He wants us to be *brothers.* The word "brother" used to bother me. It was more like a title than a love word. I guess that's because I wasn't a brother. I was a Christian but not a brother—at least not experientially. I was a step above the brother category (wherever that left me) — a supervisor of brothers, but not one of them. It wasn't because I didn't want to be; I wasn't because I didn't think I was *supposed* to be. It seemed improper for one giving "spiritual guidance" to be so transparent and vulnerable.

What I'm getting at is this: Protestants climb all over the Roman Catholics for calling their clergy class "father" because there is a Bible verse that says, "Call no man Father."[6]

But do you realize that same passage says, "Call no man leader," which blows to pieces Protestantism's "Christian Leader" syndrome. I read religious magazines and see "Christian Leaders Endorse This Insurance Plan," and I want to go "Eeeeeeeeeek!" — what are we doing! Why do we need each other to endorse our programs, when we have one leader, even Christ Jesus? Why do I need twenty-five "key" lay and clerical leaders on my board of reference, when if it is of God, it will succeed anyway?

This may sound like straining at gnats, but God's Word is specific where it needs to be specific, and it is specific here.

As you read this, is your mind telling you that what is being said is too strong and thus leads toward division instead of oneness? Not long ago, I would have agreed. But to say that involves Jesus in a moral injustice because we are dealing here with His views on sectarianism — not man's. Do not think for a moment it is easy to say these things. It wins no popularity contests, believe me. But what do we want: truth or comfort? What is our purpose: togetherness in the Lord Jesus Christ and the availing of ourselves for renewal or clinging to the vestiges of tradition so as to avoid rocking the boat?

ONENESS IS IN JESUS CHRIST

In his book, *One Body in Christ*, Japanese author Kokichi Kurosaki states, "There is only one center of Christianity, and this center is *spiritual fellowship with God through Christ — life union with God in Christ.*"[7]

In His book, *The Holy Bible*, God the Holy Spirit says, "But, telling the truth in love, we should grow up in every way toward Him who is the Head — Christ, from whom the entire body is fitted together and united.[8]

In His prayer to the Father, Jesus asked,
I am not praying only for them, but also for those who will believe in Me through their message, so that all may be one, as Thou Father art in Me, and I in Thee, so they may be in Us, and so that the world may believe that Thou hast sent Me, I have given them the glory which Thou hast given to Me, so that they may be one as We are one, I in them and Thou in Me, so that they may be completed into one, that the world may recognize that Thou hast sent Me and hast loved them as Thou hast loved Me.[9]

What is it that makes us one? The fellowship with God offered to us by Jesus Christ and preserved in us by the Holy Spirit.

Gifts are fine, but they do not make us one. Doctrine is fine, but it is not the source of oneness. The body of Jesus Christ alone is that place where oneness occurs. With Paul, I fear that our "minds should be led astray from the simplicity and purity of devotion to Christ."[10]

You may ask, "Well, if a person understands this and agrees with the Lord to be one in Him and Him alone, how are all the tendencies to stray toward other centers handled?"

I suppose my simplest answer would be, "In love, refuse them." Don't refuse the *people*, refuse *division*. Recently I was with one of my favorite brothers who, I believe, over-emphasizes a certain doctrine at the expense of the over-all picture. He knows I feel this way because I have told him so. He feels that I understate it. But it hasn't interfered with our oneness in Christ. We are completely one, have tremendous fellowship together, and our disagreements don't even count.

How I yearn for that kind of relationship with *all* believers I meet. Let me be honest and say that it is not that way yet. I have a difficult time being one with pushy Christians. It would be easy to say it is their problem, not **mine**. But Christ is one with them despite their pushiness, so I want to be one with them too. It's coming, but in this case slowly.

As the days and years pass, I predict that we will see more and more of the Holy Spirit's drawing men together in Christ and drawing them away from that which, by its inherent nature, divides—whether it *purposes* to divide or not.

When the revelation of God's call comes to you, hurt though it may, ask for grace to obey. When the structure gets in the way of your free life in Jesus, God's call is to "come away from her, My people."[11]

Before moving on to the next chapter in this book, read through John 17 to see the Lord's concern that we be one.

Seeing Ain't Believing

But the message they heard did not benefit them, because it was not united by faith to those who heard it.

— The author of the
book of Hebrews

11

Seeing Ain't Believing

When we grasp something new and real from the Lord, we often have two responses. The first is deep joy and satisfaction. We know He has spoken to us and *taught* us. But sometimes there is a second response of frustration. "If only I could see more," we say.

I cannot count the number of times I have thought to myself, after God has broken through to me on something new, "Wow—if that truth has been here all along and I have missed it up to now, how much more there must be that I have not yet perceived."

If our growth in the Spirit depended upon our ability to *see* spiritual truth, we'd all be wanting. As a matter of fact, could this not be one of our great problems today? We become "carried away" or overly concerned with what we *don't* see, as opposed to resting in what we *do* see. And it is especially true of the young in Christ.

Growth comes from God. Let me repeat it—growth comes from God. Think of how often Jesus emphasized that principle. Speaking of the Holy Spirit, the Lord said that when He would come, "*He* will guide *you* into all truth"[1] (italics mine). John 15 and the whole matter of the vine and the branches is an illustration of the fact that spiritual activity originates from God. When Peter declared that Jesus was the Christ of God, the Lord responded by saying, "It was not flesh and blood that revealed this to you but My heavenly Father."[2]

We grow in the Spirit by what God reveals to us, not by what we determine in our minds to procure from Him. Let me offer some illustrations.

When God began to show me the simplicity of the Church and the beauty of corporate life in Christ, with Him alone as Head of the body, I accepted His revelation with delight. I soon began to sense the freedom of no longer living my spiritual life under the domain of human headship, a religious habit-pattern, or things that the Lord had revealed to someone else ten or twenty years ago. Life in Christ became a clear and up-to-the-minute relationship.

Today, three years after beginning to understand these truths, things are somewhat different from what I had earlier anticipated. Since then God has taught me lessons I did not think I even *needed* to learn! Similarly, there are many things I, in my flesh, would *like* to have been shown that I don't know anything about yet.

I want to see the restoration of the Church with all my heart. The whole concept of the oneness of those who belong to Jesus Christ excites me to the core. My heart shouts "far out!" as I contemplate what the Lord must be planning.

Yet I confess aloud that I am not experiencing all I see. I look around me and I see others much farther down the pike on the issue of church life, or whatever terminology you choose to use, and I admire them. The Lord has let me admire what He is doing with other people without my getting all uptight over the fact that at this current hour He is not doing the same thing with me.

But His lovely inner peace still prevails. It's that kind of thing where you know more truth is coming but it hasn't arrived yet! And what a privilege to learn to *wait* on Jesus for His time and His means of revealing truth to us.

God's peace can prevail when we are in between growth as well as when we are growing. When you cut down a tree, you count the rings in the interior of the trunk to determine its age. The rings are there because the tree does not grow at a constant rate each day of the year. Biologists tell us that growth in a tree occurs only for a few months out of the year, and during the remainder of the time little or nothing happens.

The stock market often moves in a characteristic pattern that brokers and investors call "back and fill." When the market takes a sudden spurt upward and perhaps jumps fifty to a hundred points in a period of a few weeks, it often settles back again to the original support level and then moves upward again, this time far more steadily. Thus, it backs and fills. It shows its potential in the first move, and its solidarity in the second.

Now deliver me from patterning my life after the growth of a tree or, worse, the stock market! But in these objects I find a picture of the spiritual growth that occurs in me. I find the Lord reveals much of His truth to me in spurts, and then my experience begins to catch up with what He has shown.

Not "growing" each day used to throw me into panic. And I know other people feel that way, too, because so many of them say they do. But, really, we may be experiencing far more actual growth in these back and fill days, the in-between stages when the Lord is giving our *life* in the Spirit a chance to catch up with the *truth* of the Spirit, than we did at the actual point of reception of that truth. And in seeing this, we are released from the pressure of *having* to grow and thus are free to receive all the Lord has for us.

I don't know when He'll teach me more; I only know that He will.

Along these same lines, I have come to see there are some things in the spiritual realm I will probably never understand during this earthly trek. And by that I mean both truths that God has revealed to others—and not to me—about Himself and also the reason why certain circumstances have taken place.

Isaiah made a statement of great comfort regarding things we do not see: "For My thoughts are not your thoughts, neither are your ways My ways, says the Lord. For as the heavens are higher than the earth, so are My ways higher than your ways and My thoughts than your thoughts."[3]

As far as spiritual truth is concerned, there are some things that I will never understand and other things that the Lord may not show me for years. What a relief to know that I don't have to dig out new truth by my own effort. God's promise is that as I walk by His life, He will reveal all that I need to know.

On the other hand, as I walk with Him, I can assume He has many things for me to learn. I can expectantly wait on Him for wisdom and knowledge, for Colossians 2:3 refers to Christ "in whom all the treasures of wisdom and knowledge lie hidden." I find that knowledge from the Lord comes most often as I am fellowshiping with others who know Him. As we are together in the Lord, His Spirit will minister to us through each other.

And may I carefully make another comment: as you read His Word, allow the Holy Spirit to teach you as opposed to just trying to cram inspired facts and figures into your frontal lobe. In reading through Paul's epistles, for example, we are faced with the fact that we are reading someone else's mail — letters that were sent first to other people.

This in no way means they are not relevant to us and our needs. But it does mean that the Scripture never supersedes the Holy Spirit. It is the Spirit who guides our lives, not just words printed on a piece of paper.

When Paul tells Timothy to "not any longer drink water only, but use a little wine for the good of your stomach,"[4] this does not necessarily mean that everyone who has a fuzzy tummy should immediately imbibe the fruit of the vine.

Or when we read Jesus' words which say, "Go, therefore, and make disciples of all the nations,"[5] it does not necessarily mean that we should all immediately begin traveling so that as we go we can spread the Gospel to the entire earth. It *could* mean that for some individuals; however, the command would come from the Holy Spirit rather than just from words on a page.

Through the Scriptures the Holy Spirit will lead us into all the truth we need to know. It is not the letter itself but the Spirit's quickening the letter which gives us life.

Let me underscore the truth of Second Timothy 3:16 and 17 that "All Scripture is inspired by God and is profitable for teaching, for reproof, for correction, for training in righteousness, so that the man of God may be well-fitted and adequately equipped for all good work." However, the creation is never higher than the Creator. Since it was the Holy Spirit who superintended the writing of Scripture, He must be the One who superintends the application of His truths to our lives.

God's ways being above our ways not only means revealed truth is beyond human truth, but it also means that He will have reasons for creating circumstances in our lives which we may never understand—or need to understand.

When I was in my late twenties, I began to develop serious back trouble. My condition gradually deteriorated until I was finally unable to walk.

One evening some Christian brothers felt led to pray for me and anoint me with oil. I agreed, and as I look back on the experience, I realize that all of us sincerely expected a miracle to occur. We prayed and waited, but nothing happened. In fact, to be quite honest, the pain grew worse!

A short time later I agreed to submit to surgery, and after a four month recovery period, I was healthy again.

The Lord has never shown me for sure why He allowed this to happen. I learned a measure of patience during that ordeal, so perhaps that is the reason. Also, I was immature enough in Christ at the time that had I been healed, I might have gone off on a "healing spree," and tried to get everyone else healed according to the pattern by which God restored me. (I am not saying that to cop out on healing. I believe firmly that God does heal today through supernatural means, and I know people for whom it has happened. But so far it has not happened to me.)

Remember when the Lord took Peter, James, and John with Him to the Mount of Transfiguration?[6] The moment Jesus was surrounded with holy light and was greeted by Moses and Elijah, Peter wanted to build three tabernacles to memorialize the event. The Lord never acknowledged him, and when the encounter concluded, Jesus simply walked back down the mountain.

And still our tendency today is to "tabernacle" around something the Lord has done, assuming it needs to be repeated and permanently manifested to the world. Instead, God says to keep on walking by faith.

Suppose some day I am invited to address a service club and present what Christ means to me. I do, and several men believe and are born of God. Does that mean I should immediately rush out and begin an international ministry aimed at speaking to service clubs, endeavoring to win their members to Christ? No more so than if in losing my house and belongings through a blazing fire, and learning for the first time the sufficiency of Christ, I should seek to destroy all my future homes by fire to insure that God will keep teaching me about Christ's sufficiency.

The Father says, "The just shall live by faith."[7] Not by repetition, patterns, or following the example or experience of another (unless, of course, *He* leads you to), but by faith.

Jesus said not to worry about tomorrow.[8] He simply wants us to walk with Him today.

Recently a girl who had been on drugs told me that she did not believe she could stay off them for a period of several days. My advice to her was not to worry about the days ahead, but just let the Lord cure her problem today. She has since come to know Christ and, so far, has stayed clean. She is not concerned about being clean tomorrow; she only knows that Christ has kept her from messing up today.

The Scriptures say "we walk by faith, not by sight."[9] Seeing ain't believing. Believing is believing! As we walk with Jesus Christ each day and trust Him, He will show us all we need to see.

A Proper Time

For everything there is an appointed season, and there is a proper time for every project under heaven.

— King Solomon

12

A Proper Time

There is little doubt that we are approaching some sort of climax to history. People—both within and without the Kingdom—sense that these are significant times. God seems to be getting it all together while the world presses on in increasing confusion and desperation.

What an hour for those of us who belong to Jesus Christ to lay aside everything that holds us back and run with patience and enthusiasm the race set before us.[1] We need to break loose from our mediocrity and believe God for everything that He has!

I used to hear about people who were so heavenly minded they were no earthly good. Funny, but in my twelve years as a member of God's family, I've never met one! Could it be, instead, that we are to be heavenly minded enough to be some earthly good? It is, after all, the kingdom of heaven which will be around forever and the kingdom of this world which will fade away.

For me, life in the heavenlies gets more attractive all the time. Earthly laurels hold less meaning for me. Far more rewarding is my union with Christ and His people.

When I was a child, I used to play with toy cars. I don't do that anymore. It is not that I ever consciously gave them up—I just outgrew them. The parallel is obvious. When you see the permanence and truth of the Lord Jesus Christ and His present and future life, everything else seems like just toothpaste! What is there left to compare with the life which He offers?

Becoming a child of God is an unmatched privilege, but salvation is just the beginning. It is the starting point of God's plan. He is gathering His people and molding them as one into something that lasts forever.

He is building us together *now!* As citizens-in-advance of His great, new City, He is making us ready as His bride to occupy our new home. This is His plan which He is carrying out among us right this moment as we live together in Christ.

I have a reason to depend utterly upon the Lord Jesus which far surpasses anything I have ever known. Living our lives in abandon to Jesus Christ is done not just because God wants us to be good boys and girls but because *He is making us into something new*—a City, a Kingdom, an everlasting domain.

"There is a proper time for every project under heaven."[2] What is occurring in people's lives today is certainly no accident. Jesus said, "You will know them by the deeds they do."[3] After observing the evidences of fantastic spiritual newness and depth in the hearts of those turning to Christ, I believe with all my heart that this is God's proper time for a large-scale harvest. He is gathering a body of people to Himself who are exhibiting a tremendous depth of spiritual life. What a time to bid farewell to earth-type life!

For those of us who have believed for some time, let us exercise our free wills to trust Him—and not deter Him—as He seeks through the Holy Spirit to include us in His new works. Allow Christ to be your life. Turn away from fake world kingdoms and identities and let Jesus remake you as a citizen on high. Live at God's right hand. Stand your ground against the foe, clad in your spiritual armor, and salute the King as He seeks to build and mold a people on the offense. Avail yourself to Him as He plants new desires, new "want-to's" within you. Believe Him and watch Him never allow you to be tempted beyond what you are able to bear—never permitting you to fall out when the bottom does.

Drink of His peacefulness and tranquillity, so that as the hectic systems of man come forth to allure you into their activities, you will be so taken up with your rest in the Lord that the world's alternatives will not even approach reality. Make your allegiance to oneness, Jesus Christ and Him alone. When division comes, refuse it! Our family name as Sons of God is far too potent even to be touched or swayed by the strifes of man. And when you see a truth which is fresh and new, let it sift into your life with Christ and not just into your understanding. Be satisfied with what God reveals and be content until He chooses to show you more.

God has His proper time. His time is Now! He wants our trust and availability to permit Him to build us up into one new man in Jesus Christ.

Farewell, old man, with all your pressures, anxieties, exploitations, manipulations, depressions, and everything else about your ugly schemes which used to look so good.

Hello, Lord Jesus. I crave Your love and life! Hello, Jerusalem. What peaceful, regal beauty I see within your gates.

Hello, new man. I can really get into you because I know I am one with you. I *am* you!

Hello, fellow pilgrims. What a joy to be one with you. Let's move on from here in the power of God's Spirit and be the satisfied recipients of all He has in store for us.

Notes

Chapter 1

1. Hebrews 13:8
2. Romans 5:20
3. Paraphrase of Matthew 9:12
4. Psalm 76:10
5. According to a newscast on NBC affiliate station WMC, in Memphis, Tennessee, late in 1970.
6. UPI news release, ibid.
7. John 14:6
8. John 8:32
9. John 16:33

Chapter 2

1. Luke 18:8
2. Revelation 21:2; Ephesians 5:26,27

Chapter 3

1. Revelation 19:7
2. Revelation 20:6
3. Revelation 20:14; I Corinthians 15:26
4. Hebrews 11:10
5. Psalms 46 and 48
6. Isaiah chapters 60-62
7. Romans 11:17-24
8. John 14:1-3
9. Hebrews 9:25
10. Ephesians 2:6
11. Revelation 21:11-21
12. Revelation 22:5

Chapter 4

1. Revelation 21:2
2. Philippians 2:13
3. Philippians 1:21
4. Matthew 16:19
5. Psalm 8:6
6. Hebrews 13:14

Chapter 5

1. II Peter 1:3 (KJV)
2. See I Corinthians 15:42-55

3. Ephesians 5:30 (KJV)
4. Hebrews 1:3
5. Ibid.
6. Ephesians 2:6
7. Paraphrase of Romans 6:6
8. John 14:19 (KJV)
9. Paraphrase of Galatians 2:20 from the Greek

Chapter 6

1. I John 5:18
2. I Peter 5:8
3. John 8:44
4. Paraphrase of Genesis 3:1
5. II Corinthians 6:14
6. James 1:3
7. Romans 8:28
8. Matthew 25:41
9. Luke 10:18
10. Jude 9
11. "The Cult of the Occult," *Newsweek* April 13, 1970, pp. 96,97
12. Ibid.
13. Nicholas Pileggi, "Occult," *McCalls* March, 1970, pp. 63, 64
14. Matthew 13:19
15. I John 5:19
16. See I Peter 2:18, Titus 2:9; I Timothy 6:1
17. I Corinthians 13:8
18. John 12:31; John 16:11; Revelation 1:5
19. Matthew 4:8-10
20. II Corinthians 10:4 (KJV)
21. Ephesians 6:14
22. See the entire account in Matthew 12:22-29
23. Revelation 12:11
24. Colossians 2:15
25. James 4:7

Chapter 7

1. Romans 6:1,2
2. I Timothy 1:9
3. Psalm 37:4
4. See Ephesians 2:2,3
5. Romans 8:31

Chapter 8

1. Romans 8:28
2. Psalm 76:10
3. Hebrews 13:15 (KJV)
4. Psalm 100:4
5. Hebrews 13:5
6. Matthew 11:28
7. Ephesians 6:10
8. Philippians 4:13
9. Romans 8:38,39

Chapter 9

1. Exodus 14:14
2. II Corinthians 5:14
3. See Hebrews 9:24

Chapter 10

1. John 17:21
2. John 13:35
3. Ephesians 4:4-6
4. John 16:3
5. Proverbs 21:19
6. Matthew 23:9-11, *New American Standard Bible* (NASB), published by the Lockman Foundation.
7. Kokichi Kurosaki, *One Body in Christ*, Northridge: Voice Christian Publications, Inc., 1968, p. 26
8. Ephesians 4:15,16
9. John 17:20-23
10. II Corinthians 11:3 (NASB)
11. Revelation 18:4

Chapter 11

1. John 16:13
2. Matthew 16:17
3. Isaiah 55:8,9
4. I Timothy 5:23
5. Matthew 28:19
6. Matthew 17:1-9
7. Hebrews 10:38 (KJV)
8. See Matthew 6:34
9. II Corinthians 5:7

Chapter 12

1. See Hebrews 12:1
2. Ecclesiastes 3:1
3. Matthew 7:16